LOVE IN A
DARK TIME

COLM TÓIBÍN

LOVE IN A DARK TIME

GAY LIVES FROM WILDE TO ALMODÓVAR

PICADOR

First published 2001 by Pan Macmillan Australia Pty Limited, Sydney

This edition published 2002 by Picador
an imprint of Pan Macmillan Ltd
Pan Macmillan, 20 New Wharf Road, London N1 9RR
Basingstoke and Oxford
Associated companies throughout the world
www.panmacmillan.com

ISBN 0 330 49137 7

3 5 7 9 8 6 4 2

A CIP catalogue record for this book is available from
the British Library.

Printed and bound in Great Britain by
Mackays of Chatham plc, Chatham, Kent

FOR FINTAN O'TOOLE

CONTENTS

INTRODUCTION

IN THE AUTUMN OF 1993, AT THE EDINBURGH FESTIVAL, I arranged to meet Andrew O'Hagan, who at that time was an editor at the *London Review of Books*. I remember him knocking on my hotel room door in the late afternoon. When I answered, he walked quickly past me and across the room to the window. He stood there for some time checking out the view in all its detail. (There was nothing much to see.) And then he turned and looked at me. I had never met him before.

That night we went to a dinner in a Scottish castle where the cream of Scottish culture, some of them rich and thick, entertained us. And after that we fell into a bar somewhere in the middle of the city where we stayed until the small hours. Andrew O'Hagan drank whisky and I drank beer and slowly it emerged that there was something he wanted to ask me. The *London Review of Books*, he said, was commissioning a series of articles which would also become pamphlets and they wanted me to do one of them. These pieces would be long and serious, he said, but

also personal and polemical. I presumed as he spoke
that they wanted me to do something about Ireland
since I had been writing about Irish books and Irish
history for the *London Review of Books*. No, it wasn't
about Ireland, Andrew O'Hagan said, and he seemed
hesitant and almost embarrassed. Instead, they wondered if I would write a pamphlet about my own
homosexuality.

I told him instantly I couldn't do that. It was a matter, I said, which I did not think that I could write
about. And there were so many other writers who
could easily do so. I had, when we spoke, written the
first chapter of my novel 'The Story of the Night', in
which I dealt with homosexuality directly for the first
time, but it was set in another country and it was not
autobiographical, or not obviously so. My sexuality,
like Richard's in that novel, was something about
which part of me remained uneasy, timid and melancholy. I told him I couldn't do it. I had nothing
polemical and personal, or even long and serious to
say on the subject. He said nothing. We kept drinking
and we talked about other things.

Clearly, without my realising, the *London Review of
Books* then decided on another method of enticing me
to confront my own sexuality in print. They began to
send me books about gay writers or by gay writers,
and some of these books were too interesting to resist.
Thus between 1994 and 2000 I found myself writing
constantly on the subject not of the idea or the theory
of homosexuality for the paper, but of the work and
lives of homosexuals. The figures who interested me

most however, were not gay writers such as Edmund White, Alan Hollinghurst, David Leavitt, Michael Cunningham, Jeanette Winterson or Emma Donoghue, whose novels had done so much to clear the air and make things easier for gay people, whose bravery and honesty I viewed with a kind of awe, but other figures from an earlier time, whose legacy was ambiguous, who had suffered for their homosexuality (Oscar Wilde, Roger Casement) or had remained uneasy and secretive about it (Thomas Mann, Elizabeth Bishop), who had allowed it to nourish rather than dominate their work (James Baldwin), who had thrived in adverse conditions (Francis Bacon, Pedro Almodóvar), and who had written the elegies and memoirs during the AIDS catastrophe (Thom Gunn, Mark Doty).

This, then, is a book in the main about gay figures for whom being gay seemed to come second in their public lives, either by choice or by necessity. But in their private lives, in their own spirit, the laws of desire changed everything for them and made all the difference. The struggle for a gay sensibility began as an intensely private one, and slowly then, if the gay man or woman was a writer, or a painter or a filmmaker or a reformer, it seeped into language and images and politics in ways which were strange and fascinating. Writing these pieces helped me to come to terms with things – with my own interest in secret, erotic energy (Casement and Mann), my interest in Catholicism (Wilde and Casement converted close to the end; the work of Almodóvar is full of Catholic imagery), my interest in Irish Protestants (Wilde, Casement, Francis Bacon), my admiration for figures who, unlike myself, weren't afraid (Wilde, Bacon, Almodóvar), my abiding fascination with sadness (Bishop, Baldwin, Doty) and, indeed, tragedy (Gunn and Doty).

In the 1970s, Thomas Mann's *Doctor Faustus*, James Baldwin's *Go Tell It On The Mountain*, Thom Gunn's *My Sad Captains* and Elizabeth Bishop's *Selected Poems* were among my favourite books. But I did not know that the authors were gay until later. This book, then, reflects my excitement at that discovery and my interest in exploring their work and their lives with that new knowledge. The book is also a tentative history of progress. The first subject of this book was born in the 1850s and the book reflects the shift in tolerance between then and now: Mark Doty and Pedro Almodóvar are contemporaries of mine, born a hundred years after Oscar Wilde and living now in a less dark time.

ROAMING THE
GREENWOOD

IN HIS ESSAY 'THE ARGENTINE WRITER AND TRADITION', Borges wrote that the Argentine writer, and the South American writer, by virtue of being distant and close at the same time, had more 'rights' to Western culture than anyone in any Western nation. He went on to explore the extraordinary contribution of the Jewish artist to Western culture and of the Irish writer to English literature. For them, he argued, it was 'enough, the fact of being Irish and different, to be innovators within English culture'. Similarly, Jewish artists 'work within the culture and at the same time do not feel tied to it through any special devotion'. His essay was written around 1932, a long time before any clear view emerged of the gay writer's place in literary tradition, and before the idea emerged that Irish, Jewish or gay (or, later, South American) writing was itself the centre rather than the periphery renewing the centre.

Borges was, in many ways, a conservative man, and a cautious critic. He would have been interested in the notion that many or most of the figures who re-created modern writing were gay, or Irish, or Jewish: Melville, Whitman, Hopkins, James, Yeats, Kafka, Woolf, Joyce, Stein, Beckett, Mann, Proust, Gide, Firbank, Lorca, Cocteau, Auden, Forster, Cavafy. But he would have been slightly unsettled, I think, by the thought of the gay element in this list, and by the idea that in place of 'Irish' or 'Jewish' or 'Argentine' in his essay on tradition, you could put the word 'gay' or 'homosexual'. He would also, I think, be disturbed by the idea that you could find enough traces, or indeed direct evidence, in the work of, say, Shakespeare and Marlowe and Bacon to declare them, too, part of the gay tradition, the secret dotted line that runs right through Western literature. Yet, like most writers, Borges was obsessed with what came before him, with the books and writers – Quixote, the gaucho Martín Fierro, Flaubert, Kipling – that represented his own secret dotted line to the past. He could not have done without them.

It is easy to argue about the uncertain Irishness of certain writers. Was Sterne Irish? Was Oliver Goldsmith Irish? Was Robert Tressell Irish? Was Iris Murdoch Irish? But the argument about who was gay and who was not and how we know is more difficult. How can someone be gay if, as in the case of Gogol, there is no direct evidence? Yet if you trawl through Gogol's stories with grim determination, you will find a hidden world of signs and moments, fears and prejudices, and these can be interpreted as evidence of his homosexuality.

Why bother? Why should this matter? It matters

because as gay readers and writers become more visible and confident, and gay politics more settled and serious, gay history becomes a vital element in gay identity, just as Irish history does in Ireland, or Jewish history among Jewish people. It is not simply a question of finding obscure traces of a gay presence in the past, although there is that as well, but of including writers – Whitman is a good example – who were clearly and explicitly gay, and whose homosexuality, ignored by most critics and teachers, has a considerable bearing on their work. Straight critics have tended to write about gay writers as though they were straight, or as though it did not matter which they were. Lionel Trilling published a book on E.M. Forster's fiction in 1944. In 1972, he wrote to Cynthia Ozick that

> it wasn't until I had finished my book on Forster that I came to the explicit realisation that he was homosexual. I'm not sure whether this was because of a particular obtuseness on my part or because ... homosexuality hadn't yet formulated itself as an issue in the culture. When the realisation did come, it at first didn't seem of crucial importance, but that view soon began to change.

The gay past in writing is sometimes explicit and sometimes hidden, while the gay present is, for the most part, only explicit. Soon in the Western world being gay will no longer involve difficulty and discrimination. In some places, especially cities, this is the case even now, to the extent that the phrase 'post-gay' is slowly becoming current. Therefore, how we read the past, and read into the past, and judge the past are likely to become matters of more open debate. The temptation to make anachronistic judgments and ask anachronistic questions is hard to avoid. Why didn't Thomas Mann come out? Why didn't Forster publish *Maurice* in 1914, when he wrote it? Why didn't the American critic F.O. Matthiessen write a history of gay American writing? How come Lionel Trilling didn't realise that Forster was gay? And why are gay lives presented as tragic in so much writing? Why can't gay writers give gay men happy endings, as Jane Austen gave heterosexuals? Why is gay life often presented as darkly sensational?

The actions and attitudes of the past, even the recent past, remain almost unimaginable now, things have changed so quickly. As recently as 1970 the essayist Joseph Epstein could write the following in *Harper's* magazine:

> Private acceptance of homosexuality, in my experience, is not to be found, even among the most liberal-minded, sophisticated and liberated people. Homosexuality may be the one subject left in America about which there is no official hypocrisy . . . Cursed without clear cause, afflicted without apparent cure, they are an affront to our rationality, living evidence of our despair of ever finding a sensible, an explainable design to the world.

And if one of his four sons turned out to be gay, he continued, he 'would know them condemned to a state of permanent niggerdom among men, their lives, whatever adjustments they might make to their condition, to be lived out as part of the pain of the earth'.

In a chapter entitled 'The Pink Triangle', Gregory Woods writes:

> After the 'liberation' of the camps by the Allies, those survivors who wore the pink triangle – denoting that they had been imprisoned as homosexuals – were treated as common criminals who had deserved their incarceration. Many were transferred to prisons proper to serve out their terms . . . The pink triangle was left off Holocaust memorials . . . The Nazis had introduced a stricter version of the anti-homosexual law in Paragraph 175 of the German penal code in 1935. Unlike other Nazi laws, this was not repealed at the end of the war.

Other communities who have been oppressed – Jewish people, say, or Catholics in Northern Ireland – have every opportunity to work out the implications of their oppression in their early lives. They hear the stories; they have the books around them. Gay people, on the other hand, grow up alone; there is no history. There are no ballads about the wrongs of the past, the martyrs are all forgotten. It is as though, in Adrienne Rich's phrase, 'you looked into the mirror and saw nothing'. Thus the discovery of a history and a heritage has to be made by each individual as part of the road to freedom, or at least knowledge, but it also has serious implications for readers and critics who are not particularly concerned about gay identity, and it also has serious dangers.

Let us begin with Whitman; he is the easiest. His poem 'When I Heard at the Close of the Day' is written in one sentence. Even though the narrator hears how his 'name had been received with plaudits in the capitol', the poem tells us, it is still not a happy night for him, but 'when I thought how my dear friend my lover was on his way coming, O then I was happy' and the poem ends:

> For the one I love most lay sleeping with me
> under the same cover in the cool night,
> In the stillness in the autumn moonbeams
> his face was inclined toward me,
> And his arm lay lightly around my breast –
> and that night I was happy.

This is only one of Whitman's explicitly gay love poems. It is easy to imagine F.O. Matthiessen and his lover Russell Cheney reading it in the Twenties. Since they had no role models and no sense of being part of any tradition it was the sort of work which was important for them. Matthiessen wrote:

> Of course this life of ours is entirely new – neither of us knows a parallel case. We stand in the middle of an uncharted, uninhabited country. That there have been other unions like ours is obvious, but we are unable to draw on their experience. We must create everything for ourselves. And creation is never easy.

During the years when Matthiessen explored this 'uncharted, uninhabited country', he taught at Harvard and wrote *The American Renaissance: Art and Expression in the Age of Emerson and Whitman*, published in 1941, which became the most influential book on the subject. (His omission of Emily Dickinson has, in recent years, damaged the book's canon-forming status.) His essay on Whitman is more than a hundred pages long. He writes with great subtlety about Whitman's language, the tension between the vernacular and the abstract, the practical and the transcendental. He writes about the influences on Whitman, including opera and painting, and about the influence of Whitman on others, including Henry James – who read Whitman, he told Edith Wharton, in 'a mood of subdued ecstasy' – and Hopkins, who wrote: 'I always knew in my heart Walt Whitman's mind to be more like my own than any man living.' 'Hopkins must have been referring,' Matthiessen writes, 'to Whitman's homosexuality and his own avoidance of this latent strain in himself.' In a footnote, he quotes in full and without comment an explicitly homosexual letter from Whitman to a friend.

Fifty pages earlier, Matthiessen has also referred to Whitman's homosexuality. He is writing about a passage at the beginning of *Song of Myself*:

> *I mind how once we lay such a transparent*
> *summer morning,*
> *How you settled your head athwart my hips*

and gently turned over upon me,
And parted the shirt from my bosom-bone,
and plunged your tongue to my
bare-strip't heart,
And reach'd till you felt my beard, and
reach'd till you held my feet.

Matthiessen's commentary is vaguely disapproving of the tone of this passage. 'In the passivity of the poet's body,' he writes, 'there is a quality vaguely pathological and homosexual.' It is a sentence which, fifty years or more after it was written, burns on the page. Pathological and homosexual. Jonathan Arac, who edited Matthiessen's letters, wrote that 'to create the centrally authoritative critical identity of *American Renaissance*, much had to be displaced, or scattered, or disavowed.' Matthiessen was aware of this. In January 1930 he wrote to his boyfriend:

My sexuality bothers me, feller, sometimes when it makes me aware of the falseness of my position in the world. And consciousness of my falseness seems to sap my confidence of power. Have I any right to live in a community that would so utterly disapprove of me if it knew the facts? I hate to hide when what I thrive on is absolute directness.

'For most of his students and younger colleagues,' the *Dictionary of American Biography* says,

Matthiessen's homosexuality was suggested, if at all, only by the fact that his circle was more predominantly heterosexual than was usual in Harvard literary groups at the time and that he was unusually hostile to homosexual colleagues who mixed their academic and sexual relations.

In 1950, five years after the death of his lover, and shortly before he was due to appear before the House Un-American Activities Committee – he was also a left-wing activist – Matthiessen jumped from the twelfth floor of a Boston hotel and killed himself. He was forty-eight.

In our search for a gay heritage, it is easy to lay claim to Whitman and show how deeply influential his homosexuality was on the way he used language in his poems, but what do we do about Matthiessen? He lived two lives, and he was not alone in that; he felt deeply uncomfortable about his homosexuality and that of others, and he was not alone in that either. This is not to say that these choices were imposed on him: of course he had a choice. But it would have been difficult: it would have taken heroic courage, and there was something about Matthiessen's intelligence which was deeply suspicious of the heroic. What we have are his letters and journals and his critical work: the tone of one is clearly gay (and open and loose); the tone of the other is brilliant and academic and discloses nothing, except his fear of homosexuality. This fear belongs to us all: it is something that almost every gay person has felt at some level, at some age, in some place. The gay past is not pure (as the Irish past can often seem too pure); it is duplicitous and slippery, and it requires a great deal of sympathy and understanding.

The gay past, then, contains silence and fear as well as Whitman's poems and Shakespeare's sonnets, and this may be why the work of Kafka continues to interest gay readers so much, and why it is so easy to find a gay subtext in Kafka's novels and stories. Some critics go further, however. 'It is only when one reads the totality of Kafka's writings,' Ruth Tiefenbrun has written,

> that it becomes apparent that the predicament of all his heroes is based on the fact that they are all homosexuals . . . Since Kafka spent his entire lifetime deliberately concealing his homosexuality, it is not at all surprising that there are relatively few overt references to homosexuality in his personal letters, diaries, notebooks, or in his creative works . . . Kafka shares with his fellow deviants their most distinctive trait: their simultaneous need to conceal themselves and to exhibit themselves.

Gregory Woods in *A History of Gay Literature* considers Ruth Tiefenbrun's theories too reductive of Kafka's genius, but convincing in relation to his work. 'The question we have to ask ourselves,' he writes,

> is whether, in order to appreciate the texts in question as gay literature, we have to accept a largely speculative

narrative about the author's life . . . In short, why
should a text not be its own proof of the readings one
performs upon it?

The argument then moves from what Kafka meant,
to what Kafka really meant, to what we mean when
we read Kafka.

I think we mean a great deal. The stories and novels
dramatise the lives of isolated male protagonists who
are forced to take nothing for granted, who are in
danger of being discovered and revealed for who they
really are ('Metamorphosis'), or who are unfairly
whispered about ('Someone must have been telling lies
about Joseph K.'), or whose relations with other men
are full of half-hidden and barely-hidden and often
clear longings ('Description of a Struggle' or certain
scenes in *The Castle*). 'No other writer of our century,'
Irving Howe has written,

> has so strongly evoked the claustral sensations of
> modern experience, sensations of bewilderment, loss,
> guilt, dispossession . . . The aura of crisis hanging
> over Kafka's life and work is at once intimately sub-
> jective, his alone, and austerely impersonal, known to
> all of us.

The aura of crisis arises of course from Kafka's being
a German-speaking Jew in Prague, a genius in a bourgeois world and, for gay readers at least, if not for
Irving Howe, a homosexual. This is not to suggest
that gay readers want Kafka to be read as a gay writer

only, although some do, but as a figure whose work was sufficiently affected by his homosexuality for various parts of it to be read as a parable about a gay man in a hostile city, as well as a non-believing Jewish man, as well as a twentieth-century man.

Gregory Woods has a brilliant reading of *Nineteen Eighty-Four* which casts some doubt on this reading of Kafka. He sees Winston and Julia's illicit, furtive love affair, and the efforts of Orwell's thought police to do away with sex and sexuality, as an account of the lives of gay men in London in 1948, the year the novel was written. Woods quotes passages like this:

> He wished that he were walking through the streets with her just as they were doing now but openly and without fear, talking of trivialities and buying odds and ends for the household. He wished above all that they had some place where they could be alone together without feeling the obligation to make love every time they met.

And comments: 'Gay readers may recognise this as a murmur from the closet. Which brings us to the point.'

Woods's point is this:

> whenever I read *Nineteen Eighty-Four* I cannot help imagining, between its lines, the spectral presence of another novel, a gay novel called 'Nineteen Forty-Eight', in which two young Londoners called Winston and Julian fall in love with each other and struggle to

16

sustain their relationship under the continuous threat of blackmail, exposure and arrest.

He realises, of course, that neither Orwell nor his straight readers had any idea that the novel could be read in this way.

What read as a futuristic nightmare to the hetero-sexual reader must have seemed to the homosexual reader somewhat paranoid and ignorant, because so close to the reality of homosexual life in England at the time – but showing no sign that Orwell was aware of his fact.

The gay reader, then, especially the reader schooled in the world before Stonewall, moves subjectively among texts which deal with forbidden territory, secrecy, fear. While there is some evidence in Kafka's work that he may have been desperately trying both to hide his sexuality and at the same time deal with it, there is no such evidence in Orwell's work and, indeed, his biographers are clear and convincing on the matter of his heterosexuality in a way that Kafka's are not. Nonetheless, as Woods emphasises, the reader is the one who makes the difference.

In her *Epistemology of the Closet*, Eve Kosofsky Sedgwick writes:

it was only close to the end of the nineteenth-century that a cross-class homosexual role and a consistent, ideologically full thematic discourse of male homosexuality became entirely visible, in developments that were publicly dramatised in – though far from confined to – the Wilde trials.

Kosofsky Sedgwick is careful not to push the matter further, but other writers – Woods calls them 'Post-Foucauldian' – have taken the view that until the time of the Wilde trial there wasn't really a concept of homosexuality, even among those sexually attracted to their own sex: there were homosexual acts, but because of the lack of a visible discourse, it is difficult to know, until Wilde, what this meant, even to the individuals involved. Gregory Woods writes about Théophile Gautier's novel *Mademoiselle de Maupin*, published in 1835, in which the hero d'Albert realises that he loves a man and considers the implications of that:

> This is how a Frenchman came out to himself (and to his closest friend) in 1835. Note that he believes his life has fundamentally changed. He is not simply disturbed at the thought that he has, just this once and temporarily, been physically aroused by a man's body, nor even by that thought's implication, that he could act on that arousal and make love with the male body in question. No, the issue goes much deeper than that, and is a question of the essence of his personality, rather than just a fleeting physical aberration.

This, as Woods points out, would later be called 'homosexuality'. It can still be argued that what

Woods describes in Gautier's novel has happened to people since the beginning of time (or, perhaps more accurately, the beginning of people). Those to whom it happened were, it seems, generally sensible enough to keep it to themselves, or, indeed, to keep it away from themselves, until recent years, and ostensibly fall in with whatever sexual mores their society insisted on (in Greece and Rome relations between men of the same age and exclusive homosexuality were quite different from relations between men and boys).

Any indication given by anyone about homosexual feelings between the fall of the Roman Empire and the trial of Oscar Wilde is of enormous interest, which is why some sixteenth-century texts in English, such as the first 126 Sonnets, are important texts, as are certain scenes in Shakespeare's plays. Woods points first to the plays and asks us to consider Antonio in *The Merchant of Venice* as gay and, more convincingly, Achilles and Patroclus in *Troilus and Cressida*; and then quotes the passage from *Othello* where Iago recounts being in bed with Cassio (nothing special about that, Woods emphasises) and hearing him say 'Sweet Desdemona' and then:

> *would he gripe and wring my hand,*
> *Cry 'O sweet creature!' and then kiss me hard,*
> *As if he plucked up kisses by the roots,*
> *That grew upon my lips; then laid his leg*
> *Over my thigh, and sighed and kissed, and then*
> *Cried 'Cursèd fate that gave thee to the Moor!'*

Why, Woods asks, does Iago not push Cassio away? He does not, however, want to insist on Iago being merely a gay protagonist (that is, if he is a gay protagonist). He is really building up to the fun he is going to have with the Sonnets. He has most fun with Sonnet 20:

> A woman's face with Nature's own hand painted
> Hast thou, the master-mistress of my passion
> A woman's gentle heart, but not acquainted
> With shifting change, as is false woman's fashion;
> An eye more bright than theirs, less false in rolling,
> Gilding the object whereupon it gazeth;
> A man in hue, all hues in his controlling,
> Which steals men's eyes and women's souls amazeth.
> And for a woman wert thou first created,
> Till Nature as she wrought thee fell a-doting,
> And by addition thee of me defeated,
> By adding one thing to my purpose nothing.
> But since she prick'd thee out for women's pleasure,
> Mine be thy love, and thy love's use their treasure.

In the *Art of Shakespeare's Sonnets*, Helen Vendler points out that 'the individual letters of the word "h-e-w-s" (the Quarto spelling) or "h-u-e-s" [are] in as many lines as possible' in Sonnet 20. She also notes the 'unique case' of feminine rhymes throughout the sonnet. Woods writes that there has been considerable embarrassment among critics about this sonnet. In 1840 D.L. Richardson wrote: 'I could heartily wish that Shakespeare had never written it.' In 1963 H.M.

Young argued that Sonnet 20 'simply could not have been written by a homosexual'. How, he asked, could the one thing which Nature added – a penis – be 'nothing' to the poet if the poet were homosexual. 'It would . . . have been the one thing absolutely essential.' Not necessarily. Gregory Woods, quite rightly, points out: 'There is, after all, a lot more to a boy than his penis. What about his arse?' Eve Kosofsky Sedgwick, he writes, reminds us that 'here again as elsewhere in the Sonnets, "nothing" denotes, among other things, female genitals.' Thus, as Woods writes, the youth is 'chiefly admired for the promise of his backside'.

Woods sobers up a bit a few paragraphs later and points out that the sonnet, whether we like it or not, sexualises its object and 'constitutes a reflexive statement of the poet's coming out to himself'. The reader has a right, I think, to be uneasy about the use of a term like 'coming out' about Shakespeare and Sonnet 20, and I presume that Woods is doing this deliberately. In his chapter on Shakespeare, he quotes critics who are laden down with prejudice about homosexuality. 'Much is at stake,' he writes. 'A national poet is at far greater risk of censorious distortion than any merely good writer who happens to work in a national language.' He cites Eric Partridge in *Shakespeare's Bawdy* in 1968 beginning his argument against Shakespeare's homosexuality with the phrase 'Like most other heterosexual persons, I believe . . . ' Woods makes nonsense of Partridge's arguments. He goes on to quote Shakespeare's biographer Hesketh Pearson:

Homosexualists have done their utmost to annex
Shakespeare and use him as an advertisement of their
own peculiarity. They have quoted Sonnet 20 to
prove he was one of themselves. But Sonnet 20 proves
conclusively that he was sexually normal.

Hallet Smith said of Sonnet 20: 'The attitude of the
poet toward the friend is one of love and admiration,
deference and possessiveness, but it is not at all a sexual
passion'; Robert Giroux that the feelings in the poems
'do not represent the feelings of an active homosexual';
Peter Levi that 'homosexual love was to Elizabethans
inevitably chaste.'

Pull the other one, Peter. No one watching
Marlowe's *Edward II* could have felt for one moment
that the relationship between Edward and Gaveston
was a chaste relationship; nor could anyone watching
Edward transfer his affection to Spenser Junior in the
play have failed to accept and understand that
Edward preferred men. Mortimer Senior, in a speech
in the play, seems to believe that Edward's relationship
with Gaveston was in a long tradition, but that he
would grow out of it:

> And seeing his mind so dotes on Gaveston,
> Let him without controlment have his will.
> The mightiest kings have had their minions:
> Great Alexander loved Hephaestion;
> The conquering Hercules for Hylas wept;
> And for Patroclus stern Achilles drooped;
> And not kings only, but the wisest men.

The Roman Tully loved Octavius;
Grave Socrates, wild Alcibiades.
Then let his grace, whose youth is flexible,
And promiseth as much as we can wish,
Freely enjoy that vain light-headed earl,
For riper years will wean him from such toys.

'The sight of the instrument,' Harry Levin wrote, referring to the red-hot spit which is shoved up Edward's arse at the end of the play, 'would have been enough to raise an excruciating shudder in the audience; and subtler minds may have perceived, as does William Empson, an ironic parody of Edward's vice.' Woods has no time for this idea of subtler minds. It is, he writes, clear-cut: Lightborn 'pretends to seduce the faggot king, and then gives him what every faggot needs: a red-hot poker up the arse.' Any audience would have understood this.

The first 126 Sonnets are, for the most part, filled with a desire which is artful and playful and almost light: Marlowe's version of homosexual love was much darker. Edward is foolish and capricious; his gay lover comes to a sticky end. Edward's punishment, in all its horrifying melodrama, would have instilled fear in any member of the audience who had ever had sex with another man. It is, perhaps, the most politically incorrect moment in Elizabethan drama. It does not, to say the least, portray homosexual love in a positive light – the positive light of Shakespeare, and *Twelfth Night* in particular.

For gay writers and readers, this has become an

important issue. The literature gay men produced in the Seventies, Woods writes, often gave gay readers 'role models for use in the pursuit of the kinds of happiness that post-liberation gay life was meant to consist of'. Foucault, too, realised that happiness for homosexuals was a serious transgression and remarked: 'People can tolerate two homosexuals they see leaving together, but if the next day they're smiling, holding hands and tenderly embracing one another, then they can't be forgiven. It is not the departure for pleasure that is intolerable, it is the waking up happy.' Woods goes on:

> Gay critics made gay writers self-conscious about their sense of appropriate endings. No central gay character could be murdered or commit suicide, even if for reasons clearly represented as being other than homosexuality itself, for fear of enforcing the myth of the tragic queer.

(A modern version of *Edward II* would then have had Lightborn handing Edward a box of Quality Street or a bottle of Calvin Klein aftershave at the end of the play.)

As early as 1913 when he began *Maurice*, E.M. Forster was acutely conscious of this. He began the book when a friend of Edward Carpenter's, George Merrill, touched his backside

> gently and just above the buttocks. I believe he touched most people's. The sensation was unusual

and I still remember it, as I remember the position of a long vanished tooth. It was as much psychological as physical. It seemed to go straight through the small of my back into my ideas, without involving my thoughts.

He went to Harrogate, where his mother was taking the cure, 'and immediately began to write *Maurice*':

The general plan, the three characters, the happy ending for two of them, all rushed into my pen. And the whole thing went through without a hitch. It was finished in 1914.

A happy ending was imperative. I shouldn't have bothered to write otherwise. I was determined that in fiction anyway two men should fall in love and remain in it for the ever and ever that fiction allows, and in this sense Maurice and Alec still roam the greenwood. I dedicated it 'To a Happier Year' and not altogether vainly. Happiness is its keynote – which by the way . . . has made the book more difficult to publish. If it ended unhappily, with a lad dangling from a noose or with a suicide pact, all would be well . . . but the lovers get away unpunished and consequently recommend crime.

More than forty years later, Forster was still concerned about the ending of the book, and he rewrote it, leaving it happy, but more plausible. (The lovers no longer live together in a woodcutter's hut.)

The idea that gay writing has a tendency to deal in

the tragic and the unfulfilled, a tendency which Forster and writers after Stonewall sought to counteract, has echoes in Irish writing, which seems at its most content when there is a dead father or a dead child (Leopold Bloom's father committed suicide; his son is dead) and domestic chaos. No Irish novel ends in a wedding. Images of domestic bliss occur in novels like *The Vicar of Wakefield* (1766) and Roddy Doyle's *The Snapper* (1989), only to be mercilessly destroyed. The strongest images in Irish fiction, drama and poetry are of brokenness, death, destruction. The plays are full of shouting, the poetry is full of elegy, the novels are full of funerals.

There is something heroic in Forster's refusal in *Maurice* to insist that Scudder does not get arrested, or hang himself, or go to Buenos Aires. Instead, he meets Maurice again and says: 'And now we shan't be parted no more, and that's finished.' Yet somehow it isn't satisfying, any more than it would be if Leopold Bloom had been happily married and was wandering around Dublin leading his son by the hand. It would be heartening and hopeful, and politically correct, but it would not fulfil another truth which has nothing to do with hope or politics. This truth may change, of course, as gay lives change and Ireland changes; and then unhappy endings, dead children and mad old fathers may seem tagged on for reasons which have nothing to do with the truth which art requires.

In the meantime it seems to me that the two best books by gay writers published in the Nineties (and among the best published by any writers in any category during this period) take the form of elegies for gay men who died of AIDS. They are Thom Gunn's *The Man with Night Sweats* and Mark Doty's *My Alexandria*. Both books portray a world which Forster would have marvelled at, where gay happiness – *pace* Foucault – is the norm.

> *If endlessness offered itself to me today*
> *I don't think I'd have done anything*
>
> *differently*

Doty writes. There are images in both books of gay life as much as gay death: lovers and friends, gay sex and gay society. But there is an elegiac edge to every line, every moment of life described has a sense of a sad ending; the freedom of gay life is seen both as an extraordinary gift and as a tragedy. Gregory Woods quotes the *Economist* reviewer acknowledging that he or she was unimpressed by Gunn's 1982 collection *The Passages of Joy*, because 'it deals with homosexuality happily', whereas *The Man with Night Sweats*, published ten years later, 'has given his poetry more life and more raw human vigour than it ever had before'. Woods thinks that Gunn's two collections before *The Man with Night Sweats* are 'equally good'. I don't agree with this; the poems in *The Man with Night Sweats* are outstanding, not for their 'life' or 'raw human vigour', whatever that is, but for the play between the wounded elegiac voice and the poems' formal, almost impersonal tone. And maybe also because they satisfy in me an urge to have gay lives represented as tragic, an urge which I know I should repress.

'Something extraordinary began happening to [Henry] James in the mid-1890s, and more frequently in the next decade,' Fred Kaplan wrote in his biography of James. He began to fall in love with young men. 'James's sexual self-consciousness,' Kaplan continued, 'seemed either impossibly innocent or embarrassingly explicit.' 'I want in fact more of you,' he wrote to Morton Fullerton, one of the young men. 'You are dazzling . . . you are beautiful; you are more than tactful, you are tenderly, magically tactile. But you are not kind. There it is. You are not kind.'

There is no evidence that James had a physical relationship with any of these men. In *Henry James: The Young Master*, however, Sheldon Novick gives an oddly convincing account of an affair that James may have had with Oliver Wendell Holmes, the future Supreme Court judge, in 1865 when he was twenty-two and Holmes twenty-four. Novick goes on to show how James strove to match Holmes with his cousin Minnie Temple: echoes of Kate Croy and Madame Merle withholding an interesting and useful fact from an innocent young American woman about to fall in love.

James was fascinated by the life of John Addington Symonds, about whom he heard regularly from Edmund Gosse, and when there was some suggestion that Symonds might be homosexual, he told Gosse that he was 'devoured with curiosity as to this further revelation. Even a postcard (in covert words) would relieve the suspense.' In 1893 Gosse gave him one of the fifty copies of Symonds's privately printed *A Problem in Modern Ethics*, which made a case for homosexuality on the basis of its moral acceptability and aesthetic value. When a two-volume biography of Symonds appeared after his death, James read it 'with singular interest . . . There ought to be a first-rate article – a really vivid one – about him – he is a subject that would so lend itself. But who's to write it? I can't; though I should like to.'

In 1892, James had dinner with 'the morally-alienated wife of the erratic John Addington' and this gave him the idea for his story 'The Author of Beltraffio', in which a young American visits a famous author whose wife is repelled by the moral tone of his work. 'He could not control the expression of his deepest feelings in his art,' Kaplan wrote. 'Two of his powerful short stories, "The Author of Beltraffio" and "The Pupil" express the homoerotic sensuality that had no other outlet.'

The problem is that they don't. It is astonishing how James managed to withhold his homosexuality from his work. It is also astonishing how bad some of the stories are, how fey and allusive and oddly incomplete, even stories written during the years he was working on the great last novels. Thanks to a series of hints about Rome and Greece and Florence it is possible for the reader to believe that Mark Ambient, the author in 'Beltraffio', has dealt with gay subjects in his masterpiece, which is why his wife is so upset. It is also possible to believe that the American narrator, who admires Ambient so much, is gay. But it is equally possible that Ambient's book is not about gay subjects and that the narrator is not gay. Mark Ambient is married and has an extremely beautiful young son. It is possible that his wife fears for her son because of his father's sexuality. But in the story she is merely afraid that the son will read his father's work. And because the son is so young, this is not credible. So, too, with 'The Pupil'. Pemberton has come to work for the Moreen family to tutor their precocious and sickly (and quite incredible) son. The family doesn't pay him, but he stays on because he loves the boy. There is no suggestion that he fancies the boy or that he is gay. You can read that into the story if you like, but it is not in the text.

James could have altered the entire meaning of these two stories by adding a few sentences, or even a few words. But then he would have had to start again. By choosing not to add these words, he left himself with no opportunity to dramatise the scene he imagined since he could not even make it clear. He was, in his life and his work, so deliberate, so careful to control, that he could have left out anything he chose from his fiction. 'The Author of Beltraffio' and 'The Pupil' are interesting in that he came close to losing that control, but lost the stories instead.

Critics will not give up on James. He was gay; therefore he must have written stories which, if we read them carefully and deeply, will yield evidence of this. On the subject of Miles's expulsion from his school in *The Turn of the Screw*, Woods asks: 'And was what each boy whispered not only *to* boys he liked but *about* the very topic of liking boys?' And then replies: 'These can only be suspicions.' Why bother asking the question? The reason *The Turn of the Screw* works is that several possibilities are allowed to breathe fully in the story: the narrator may be mad, utterly unreliable, or Peter Quint may have truly and even sexually corrupted Miles, or both. A gay subtext is not hinted at and then withdrawn as it is in the 'The Author of Beltraffio' or 'The Pupil'; it is fully allowed. What makes this easier is that the gay subtext offers images of pure evil, whereas the nice narrator and the genius in 'The Author of Beltraffio' would both have to be gay; as would the nice teacher and the sickly boy in 'The Pupil'. It should be remembered that in 1885 the Criminal Law Amendment Bill was passed which offered two years' hard labour for private consensual homosexual acts. It is not difficult to imagine Henry James's attitude towards hard labour.

In the three James stories mentioned, young boys with striking looks, young angels, die at the end. Perhaps in 1910 and 1911, when James was in analysis with a disciple of Freud, he found out what he meant when he wrote these stories, but he left us no clue. (Thomas Mann's family could not understand why he used his adored grandson as a model for the child he so cruelly killed off in *Doctor Faustus*.) A fourth story of James's, 'The Beast in the Jungle', which comes very close to being a masterpiece, has also been interpreted as having a gay theme.

In *Epistemology of the Closet*, Eve Kosofsky Sedgwick has an interesting essay on James and 'The Beast in the Jungle'. It is possible, she writes, that critics believed that James himself translated 'lived homosexual desires, where he had them, into written heterosexual ones so thoroughly and so successfully that the difference makes no difference, the transmutation leaves no residue.' She herself, on the other hand, believes that James 'often, though not always, attempted such a disguise or transmutation, but reliably left a residue both of material that he did not attempt to transmute and of material that could be transmuted only rather violently and messily'.

When, in 'The Beast in the Jungle', May Bartram meets John Marcher, she remembers the 'secret' he has told her ten years earlier. 'You said you had from your earliest time, as the deepest thing within you, the sense of being kept for something rare and strange, possibly prodigious and terrible, that was sooner or later to happen.' Eve Kosofsky writes: 'I would argue that to the extent that Marcher's secret has *a* content, the content is homosexual.'

I would argue, on the other hand, that Marcher's secret clearly has a content and the content is possibly homosexual. The problem with the story is that the 'secret' itself, the 'something rare and strange' sounds laughable when we hear it first, a heavy-handed self-dramatisation which Marcher's character in the story takes a while to recover from. The reader has a right to expect, as the years go by, either that Marcher's secret will turn out to be a delusion in which May Bartram has all along encouraged him, or that some catastrophe will actually befall him before the story ends. It is as though some traces of Kafka had arrived in Lamb House. There are only two characters in the story, both isolated, oddly neurotic; and before she dies May intimates that she knows what the 'secret' is, and it refers to something that has already happened. After her death, Marcher, too, realises, vaguely, what it is about. He has failed to love; he has been unable to love. Clearly, he has been unable to love May Bartram, as James was unable to love Constance Fenimore Woolson; and it is open to readers whether or not they believe that May has understood all along something Marcher cannot entertain. He may have failed to love her because he was gay. And because he could not deal with his own sexuality, he failed to love anybody. This, Kaplan points out, is 'an embodiment of James's nightmare vision of never having lived, of having denied love and sexuality'.

The story becomes much darker when you know about James's life – something that almost never happens with the novels. You realise that the catastrophe the story led you to expect was in fact the very life that James chose to live, or was forced to live. 'In all his work,' Leon Edel wrote, 'there is no tale written with greater investment of personal emotion.' In 'The Beast in the Jungle', James's solitary existence is shown in its most frightening manifestation: a life of pure coldness.

The story includes the sentence: 'He had been a man of his time, *the* man, to whom nothing on earth was to have happened.' Eve Kosofsky Sedgwick writes: 'The denial that the secret has a content – the assertion that its content is precisely a lack – is a stylish and "satisfying" Jamesian formal gesture.' But it is not a stylish or satisfying formal gesture. It is, ostensibly, about a man who realises that his failure to love has been a disaster; but it is also, for readers familiar with Edel's or Kaplan's biographies of James, and readers willing to find clues in the text itself, about a gay man whose sexuality has left him frozen in the world. It is, in all its implications, a desolate and disturbing story, James's 'most modern tale', according to Edel. 'No passion had ever touched him for this was what passion meant. He had seen outside of his life, not learned it from within.'

A History of Gay Literature: The Male Tradition by Gregory Woods, Yale

OSCAR WILDE:

LOVE IN A DARK TIME

THE FIRST TWO MONTHS OF 1895 WERE BUSY FOR Oscar Wilde. In late January he was in Algiers with Alfred Douglas. He wrote to Robert Ross: 'There is a great deal of beauty here. The Kabyle boys are quite lovely. At first we had some difficulty procuring a proper civilized guide. But now it is all right and Bosie and I have taken to haschish [sic]: it is quite exquisite: three puffs of smoke and then peace and love.' On Sunday, 27 January, André Gide, also in Algiers, was, according to his own account of this, checking out of the Grand Hotel d'Orient when he saw the names Oscar Wilde and Alfred Douglas on the slate in which guests' names were written. Their names were at the bottom, which meant that they must have just arrived. His was at the top, in one of his versions of the story; it was beside Wilde's in another. In any case, he later wrote that he took the sponge and wiped his name out and he made his way quickly to the station.

Gide, who was twenty-five, had met Wilde before in Paris and Florence. He left three accounts of their meeting in Algiers; some of these were later hotly denied by Alfred Douglas. The first, written the next day, was to his mother. He explained to her that he had, after much consideration the previous day, decided to return to the hotel and miss his train, as he did not want Wilde to think he was avoiding him. 'This terrible man,' he wrote,

the most dangerous product of modern civilization – still, as in Florence, accompanied by the young Lord Douglas, the two of them put on the Index in both London and Paris and, were one not so far away, the most compromising companions in the world.

Wilde, he wrote, was

charming, at the same time; unimaginable, and, above all, a very great personality. I was very lucky to have seen so much of him and to have known him so well in Paris a few years ago; that was his prime, and he will never be as good again . . . It's impossible to gauge what is the young Lord's intrinsic worth; Wilde seems to have corrupted him to the very marrow of his bones.

Two days later, Gide wrote once more to his mother:

One sees characters like this in a Shakespeare play. And Wilde! Wilde!! What more tragic life is there than his! If only he were more careful – if he were capable of being careful – he would be a genius, a great genius. But as he says himself, and knows: 'I have put my genius into my life; I have only put my talent into my works. I know it and that is the great tragedy of my life.' That is why those who have known him well will always have that shudder of terror when he is around, as I always do . . . I am happy to have met him in such a distant place, though even Algiers isn't far enough away for me to be able to face him without a certain fear; I told him so to his face . . . If Wilde's plays in London didn't run for three hundred performances, and if the Prince of Wales didn't attend his first nights, he would be in prison and Lord Douglas as well.

André Gide did not tell his mother what really happened to him in Algiers. He recounted it in *Si le grain ne meurt*, written twenty-five years later, and he said that it was the turning point in his life. Wilde took Gide to a café in a remote part of the city. Alfred Douglas having gone to Biskra in search of a boy called Ali. As tea was being prepared for them, Gide noticed 'a marvelous youth' at the half-opened door. 'He remained there quite a while, one raised elbow propped up against the door-jamb, outlined against the blackness of the night.' When Wilde called him over, he sat down and began to play a reed flute. Wilde told Gide that he was Bosie's boy.

He had an olive complexion; I admired the way his fingers held his flute, the slimness of his boyish figure, the slenderness of the bare legs that protruded from his billowing white shorts, one of the legs folding back and resting on the other knee.

As they left the café, Wilde asked Gide if he wanted the boy. Gide nervously said that he did. Wilde, having made the arrangements, laughed uproariously as his suspicions about Gide's sexuality were confirmed. They both had a drink in a hotel and then made their way to a building where Wilde had a key to an apartment. The flute-player arrived, as did another musician for Wilde.

Gide held in his

> bare arms that perfect, wild little body, so dark, so ardent, so lascivious . . . After Mohammed had left me, I remained for a long time in a state of quivering jubilation and, although I had already achieved sensual delight five times while with him, I rekindled my ecstasy a number of times after he had gone and, back in my hotel room, prolonged its echoes until morning . . . Since then, whenever I have sought pleasure, it is the memory of that night I have pursued.

Nothing again, it seems, was ever so much fun for Gide. He subsequently met up with Douglas, who had Ali in tow, dressed like Aladdin, and aged, Gide told his mother, twelve or thirteen. All three stayed in the Hotel Royal in Biskra. In his conversations with Gide, Douglas 'returned incessantly, and with disgusting obstinacy to things I spoke of only with the greatest embarrassment – an embarrassment that was increased by his total lack of it.' And yet Gide wrote that he found Douglas 'absolutely charming'.

Wilde left Algeria on 31 January 1895 to attend rehearsals of *The Importance of Being Earnest*, which opened on 14 February. The incoming ferry was twenty hours late because of a storm, and the crossing of the Mediterranean was rough. He stopped in Paris on his way to London and saw Degas, who repeated to him a comment he had made on the opening of a Liberty's shop in Paris: 'So much taste will lead to prison.'

The Importance of Being Earnest would be Wilde's second opening that year. On 3 January *An Ideal Husband* had opened with the Prince of Wales, Balfour and Chamberlain in the audience. It was an enormous success. In London in early February Wilde attended rehearsals of *The Importance of Being Earnest*, being persuaded by George Alexander, the actor-manager, who was producing the play and performing in it, to drop the last act in which Algernon is arrested for debt. This play was also a huge success, both with critics and audiences. The *New York Times* announced: 'Oscar Wilde may be said to have at last, and by a single stroke, put his enemies under his feet.'

There is no evidence that Wilde went home to his wife and children on his return from Algiers; he seems to have remained in various hotels in London. Around the 17 February he wrote to Douglas, who was returning from Algiers, that, on his arrival, 'you will of course stay with me till Saturday. I then return to Tite Street, I think.' Tite Street was the family home; he did not return there.

The spectre of Oscar Wilde haunted Henry James in the first two months of 1895, and James's correspondence during this time gives us a much richer sense than Wilde's does of what the opening of a new play could mean at the turn of the nineteenth century. 'Who shall deny the immense authority of the theatre,' he wrote, 'or that the stage is the mightiest of modern engines?' James's play *Guy Domville* opened in St James Theatre (where it was followed by *The Importance of Being Earnest*) on 5 January, and was also produced by George Alexander, who obtained the rights to Wilde's play only because the James play had failed. 'All my happiness,' James wrote to Lady Lewis on 15 December, 'is undermined by the nervousness and exhaustion (to speak frankly) consequent upon the rehearsals of my play at St James's.' On the opening night of his play, James had 'the luminous idea' of sitting through *An Ideal Husband* at the Haymarket nearby, which had opened two days earlier. 'This is a time,' he wrote to his brother, 'when a man wants a religion.'

'I sat through it,' he wrote,

> and saw it played with every appearance (so far as the crowded house was an appearance) of complete success, and *that* gave me the most fearful apprehension. The thing seemed to me so helpless, so crude, so bad, so clumsy, feeble and vulgar . . .

His own play was a disaster and the crowd, the people who had paid for their seats, booed him when he appeared on stage. 'The vulgar, the altogether brutish rumpus the other night,' he wrote to Morton Fullerton, 'over my harmless and ingenious little play was the abomination of an hour – and an hour only. Deep and dark is the abyss of the theatre.' On the night his play closed James wrote to the actress Elizabeth Robins, to whom Oscar Wilde wrote several admiring letters: 'It has been a great relief to feel that one of the most detestable incidents of my life has closed.' On 22 February James wrote to his brother: 'Oscar Wilde's farce which followed Guy Domville is, I believe, a great success – and with his two roaring successes running now at once he must be raking in the profits.'

At the same time, possibly the same day, Wilde wrote to George Alexander asking for more money.

> I am already served with writs for £400, rumours of prosperity having reached the commercial classes, and my hotel is loathsome to me. I want to leave it . . . I am sorry my life is so marred and maimed by extravagance. But I cannot live otherwise.

Wilde now attracted envy and praise instead of the mockery and the contempt he was used to from the public and the press; he had full houses in two London theatres; his exotic foreign travel and the loathsome hotel helped further to unsettle him. From everything we know of him in those two months, it is easy to conclude that his spirit, his uneasy and ambiguous sense of himself, knew no rest. Even had he not been involved with Alfred Douglas and his father, it is likely that any decision he made at this time would have been misguided.

Wilde's relationship with both Douglas and Douglas's father, the Marquess of Queensberry, is well-documented in his letters. Another crucial aspect of the story, however, is almost entirely missing. His letters to his wife Constance were destroyed; only three survive. One is from 1884, the year of their marriage, written from Edinburgh.

O execrable facts, that keep our lips from kissing, though our souls are one . . . I feel your fingers in my hair, and your cheek brushing mine. The air is full of the music of your voice, my soul and body seem no longer mine, but mingled in some exquisite ecstasy with yours. I feel incomplete without you. Ever and ever yours Oscar.

The tone of the second is rather different. It was written in February 1895, when the trouble was beginning:

Dear Constance, I think Cyril [their son, aged ten] better *not* come up. I have so telegraphed to Mr Badley [his headmaster]. I am coming to see you at nine o'clock. Please be in – it is important. Ever yours Oscar.

The third was written in April 1895, possibly on the last day of Queensberry's trial, and read:

Dear Constance, Allow no one to enter my bedroom or sittingroom – except servants – today. See no one but your friends. Ever yours Oscar.

Alfred Douglas stayed in Algiers until 18 February, so he missed the opening night of *The Importance of Being Earnest*. His father, the Marquess of Queensberry, planned to be there, however. 'Bosie's father is going to make a scene tonight,' Wilde wrote. 'I am going to stop him.' Wilde wrote to the manager of the St James Theatre asking him to write to Queensberry saying that 'you regret to find that the seat given to him was already sold, and return him his money. This will prevent trouble, I hope.' Thus Queensberry was prevented from addressing the first-night audience and making a scene. Instead, 'he left a grotesque bouquet of vegetables' for Wilde and 'prowled about for three hours, then left chattering like a monstrous ape.'

Wilde had wanted to stay in London for the rehearsals of *The Importance of Being Earnest*, but had, on Douglas's insistence, gone to Algiers. Wilde wrote to Ada Leverson: 'I begged him to let me stay to rehearse, but so beautiful is his nature that he declined at once.' On Douglas's return to London, he came to stay with Wilde at the Avondale Hotel in Piccadilly, and they both ran up a bill of £140, the hotel impounding Wilde's luggage until he paid. When Douglas proposed inviting a young friend to stay with him and Wilde refused, Douglas departed to another hotel.

On 18 February, as his son travelled back from
Algiers, the Marquess of Queensberry left the famous
card for Wilde with the note: 'To Oscar Wilde posing
as a somdomite [*sic*]' at Wilde's club, which Wilde did
not receive until 28 February. There is something
strange about Wilde's tone in his first response. His letters, up to this point, either seek to advance his career
(and the tone much of the time is shameless) or are
written in a tone, also shameless, but flippant and
mocking and funny. The letter to Robert Ross, however, written from the Hotel Avondale on 28 February
1895 has a new tone, which will slowly become that of
the last five years of Wilde's life. It is petulant and self-
pitying; it lacks all the style, irony and sense of mischief
which Wilde had been working on for twenty years. It
is as though he has ceased to be his Platonic conception
of himself and become merely Sir William Wilde's son,
full of his own importance and only too ready to be
wronged.

> Dearest Bobbie, Since I saw you something has hap-
> pened. Bosie's father has left a card at my club with
> hideous words on it. I don't see anything now but a
> criminal prosecution. My whole life seems ruined by
> this man. The tower of ivory is assailed by the foul
> thing. On the sand is my life spilt. I don't know what
> to do.

What to do seemed very clear. Robert Ross told him
to take no action. And it is significant that Wilde did,
in fact, consider going to Paris but was prevented

from doing so by the London hotel manager because he had not paid his bill. He was not wholehearted in his search for justice, or indeed disgrace. Douglas, however, was mad for action. A few weeks later, when Wilde and Douglas had returned from a stay in Monte Carlo and when it was clear that Queensberry was in possession of compromising letters, Wilde met Frank Harris and George Bernard Shaw at the Café Royal. When Harris vehemently sought to persuade him to drop the case and leave the country and Shaw agreed, Wilde seemed to be coming around to their view. ('You are sure to lose it,' Harris told him. 'You haven't a dog's chance and the English despise the beaten.') Just then, however, Douglas arrived and berated Harris for his advice. When Douglas stormed out of the restaurant, Wilde followed, saying 'It is not friendly of you, Frank, it really is not friendly.' He was not going to take their advice. Later, in 'De Profundis' Wilde went over what happened:

On our return to London those of my friends who really desired my welfare implored me to retire abroad, and not to face an impossible trial. You imputed mean motives to them for giving such advice, and cowardice to me for listening to it. You forced me to stay to brazen it out, if possible, in the box by absurd and silly perjuries. At the end, I was, of course, arrested and your father became the hero of the hour.

How somebody as worldly and bright as Wilde was, so alert to the laws of the ruling class, at the receiving end of so much advice, so vulnerable to blackmail and so broke, could have been led so easily towards his downfall remains a mystery. But there are crucial aspects of his own make-up and background, especially in the quality of his allegiances, which made him different. And there is also his strange and fierce attachment to Alfred Douglas. Both of these require explanation.

The Wildes were part of a small breed of Irish Protestants, who in the second half of the nineteenth century supported the cause of Irish nationalism, and yet remained, within Ireland, members of a ruling class and were comfortable also with the governing classes in London. Their addiction to the cause of Irish freedom gave them an edge, lifted them out of their own circumstances and gave them an astonishing individuality and independence of mind. Out of that we get the poems of Yeats and the journals of Lady Gregory. Out of that too we get Sir William Wilde and his wife.

'Of late years,' Yeats wrote in 'The Trembling of the Veil' (1922), 'I have often explained Wilde to myself by his family history.' Yeats recounted an old Dublin riddle: Question: 'Why are Sir William Wilde's nails so black?' Answer: 'Because he has scratched himself.' 'They were famous people,' Yeats wrote,

and there are many like stories; and even a horrible folk story . . . that tells how Sir William Wilde [who

was an eye surgeon] took out the eyes of some man
. . . and laid them upon a plate, intending to replace
them in a moment, and how the eyes were eaten by a
cat . . . The Wilde family was clearly of the sort that
fed the imagination of Charles Lever, dirty, untidy,
daring . . . and very imaginative and learned.

Lady Wilde, Yeats wrote,

longed always perhaps, though certainly amid much
self-mockery, for some impossible splendour of character and circumstance . . . I think her son lived with
no self-mockery at all an imaginary life; perpetually
performed a play which was in all things opposite of
all that he had known in childhood and early youth.

Lady Wilde wrote poetry under the name Speranza,
telling a fellow poet:

You, and other poets, are content to express only
your little soul in poetry. I express the soul of a great
nation. Nothing less would content me, who am the
acknowledged voice in poetry of all the people of
Ireland.

She was much given to grandiloquence.

I should like to rage through life – this orthodox
creeping is too tame for me – ah, this wild rebellious
ambitious nature of mine. I wish I could satiate it
with Empires, though a Saint Helena were the end.

Her patriotic poems were published in the *Nation*, which was founded in 1842 and had become the publication which most ignited and inflamed Irish nationalism.

In 1848 when Gavan Duffy, the editor of the *Nation*, was imprisoned, and Lady Wilde got the chance to write two editorials, she could not contain herself. In the first of them, she said that 'the long pending war with England has actually commenced' and in the other she said 'O! for a hundred thousand muskets glimmering brightly in the light of heaven.' This was included among the charges against Gavan Duffy, the government having decided not to charge Speranza. She, however, attended the trial and roared from the gallery when the articles were mentioned, declaring that she had written them.

When she married William Wilde in 1852, he already had three acknowledged illegitimate children. (The mother, according to John Butler Yeats, was the keeper of a 'black oak shop' in Dublin.) 'I wonder what Lady Wilde thought of her husband?' Yeats wrote to his son in 1921. 'When she was Miss Elgee, Mrs Butt found her with her husband [the barrister and political activist Isaac Butt who had defended Gavan Duffy] when her circumstances were not doubtful, and told my mother about it – so that she could afford to be wise and tolerant.'

William Wilde's nationalism was milder than his wife's. In his first book, *A Voyage to Madeira, Teneriffe and the Mediterranean*, written when he was twenty-five, he spoke of himself as an Englishman.

Later he accepted the post invented specially for him as Surgeon Oculist in Ordinary to the Queen. (She must not have known about his dirty fingernails.) He accepted a knighthood in 1864.

Many accounts were subsequently written of the Wildes entertaining in their house in Merrion Square. George Bernard Shaw remembered William Wilde

> dressed in stuffy brown; and as he had the sort of skin that never looks clean, he produced a dramatic effect beside Lady Wilde (in full fig) if being, like Frederick the Great, Beyond Soap and Water, as his Nietzschean son was beyond Good and Evil.

Henry Furness wrote that

> Lady Wilde, had she been cleaned up and plainly and rationally dressed, would have made a remarkably fine model of the Grand Dame, but with all her paint and tinsel and tawdry tragedy-queen get-up she was a walking burlesque of motherhood. Her husband resembled a monkey, a miserable-looking little creature, who apparently unshorn and unkempt, looked as if they had been rolling in the dust . . . Opposite to their pretentious dwelling in Dublin were the Turkish Baths, but to all appearances [neither] Sir William nor his wife walked across the street.

These accounts were all written many years later – Furness's in 1923; Shaw's in 1930. They do not tally with contemporary accounts of the Wildes which show that they were respected and admired. Sir William's three early children remained a secret; he was considered one of the most eminent eye doctors of his age; his work as an antiquarian and chronicler of the Irish landscape and Irish folklore was an important and meticulous contribution to the growing awareness of an ancient Ireland. Also, Lady Wilde's involvement with the *Nation* was viewed as an aspect of her seriousness; her poetry and her translations were much praised. The company of both Sir William and his wife was in great demand, and their Saturday afternoons were attended by more than a hundred people.

Their position in the city changed somewhat in 1864 when Oscar was nine. A patient of William's called Mary Travers had begun to claim that the doctor had given her chloroform and raped her. When Lady Wilde wrote a letter abusing her, Mary Travers sued for libel. She won a farthing damages; and while the legal costs were high, Wilde won the support of the medical establishment. He continued practising as a doctor and in 1867 produced what Richard Ellmann considered his most cheerful book, *Lough Corrib*. In 1873 the Royal Academy of Ireland conferred on him its highest honour.

The Wildes, then, lived inside the established world and outside it. They had no difficulty with his knighthood, just as Lady Wilde never repudiated her fiery editorials. (Although she did withdraw from what passed for political activity in the Ireland of the 1860s and 1870s). They were an essential part of Dublin society at the height of Victoria's rule, yet they both (him more than her) flaunted the rules of sexual morality. And neither of them managed to be discreet. Their allegiance was to an Ireland which had not yet come into place, a dream-Ireland of her poetry and his antiquarianism; their allegiance was also to their own sense of privilege and power which derived from the very oppressor of the ancient culture which they both admired. Their dual mandate, the ambiguity of their position, seemed to loosen them both, allowed them to be noticed and remembered, allowed them to do whatever they liked, and allowed Lady Wilde in 1879, when her husband had died, to follow her son and move her salon to London.

In all of Oscar Wilde's letters which refer to his mother, there is not one word of mockery or disloyalty. Mostly he refers to her not as his mother, but as Lady Wilde. He seems in his early letters to enjoy referring to her in all her grandeur. He set about promoting her work whenever he could. To his English friends whom he met at Oxford, he also set about doing an imitation of a perfectly law-abiding member of the group. In August 1876 when he was twenty-two he wrote to William Ward about their contemporary Charles Todd, later chaplain to the Royal Navy:

> In our friend Todd's ethical barometer, at what height is his moral quicksilver? Last night I strolled into the theatre about ten o'clock and to my surprise saw Todd and young Ward the quire boy in a private box together, Todd very much in the background ... I

wonder what young Ward was doing with him.
Myself I believe Todd is extremely moral and only
mentally spoons the boy, but I think he is foolish to go
about with one, if he is bringing this boy about with
him . . . He (Todd) looked awfully nervous and
uncomfortable.

In these early letters he is a clean-living Greek scholar,
travelling with his professor, or sending his poems out
to magazines, or going to his father's house in the west
of Ireland to fish, or making sure, after his father's death
in 1876, that the rents on property outside Dublin are
'to be paid to me direct'. The only things he flirted with
were Catholicism and, when he was twenty-four, [with]
Florence Balcombe. When she became engaged to Bram
Stoker and wanted one last meeting with Wilde, he
wrote her a letter in a tone more pompous than Lady
Bracknell at the height of her powers:

As for my calling at Harcourt Street, you know, my
dear Florence, that such a thing is quite out of the
question: it would have been unfair to you, and me,
and to the man you are going to marry, had we met
anywhere else but under your mother's roof, and with
your mother's sanction. I am sure that you will see
this yourself on reflection; as a man of honour I could
not have met you except with the full sanction of your
parents and in their house.

A year later, when he was installed in London, a
new, less earnest tone entered the letters. 'My dear

Harold,' he wrote to Harold Boulton, who, at twenty, was five years younger than Wilde.

> I often have beautiful people to tea, and will always be very glad to see you and introduce you to them. Any night you like to go to the theatre I will give you a bed with great pleasure in this untidy and romantic house.

Over the next two years, he moved back and forth from being worldly to being world-weary. In the summer of 1881 he wrote to Matthew Arnold:

> for, I have only now, too late perhaps, found out how all art requires solitude as its companion, only now indeed know the splendid difficulty of this great art in which you are a master illustrious and supreme.

He enclosed his first book of poems.

He moved easily among the great and the good, writing to George Curzon, also five years his junior, to thank him for defending him at the Oxford Union. 'You are a brick!' the letter began. In 1883 he wrote again to Curzon, who had returned from the East, hoping 'you have brought back strange carpets and stranger gods.' He promoted himself effortlessly. He wrote to Oscar Browning: 'If you get the opportunity, and would care for it, I wish you would review my first volume of poems about to appear.' And to Robert Browning: 'Will you accept from me the first copy of my poems – the only tribute I can offer you in return for the delight and wonder which the strength and splendour of your work has given me from my boyhood.' In the autumn of 1881 he wrote to Ellen Terry: 'Dear Miss Ellen Terry, Will you accept the first copy of my first play, a drama on modern Russia [*Vera*]? Perhaps some day I shall be fortunate enough to write something worthy of your playing.' Within a few months he was writing 'My dear Nellie, I wish you every success tonight' and ending 'your affectionate friend'.

The priggish youth who wrote to Florence Balcombe became the flirtatious young man who wrote to Harold Boulton and then became the young poet who sent flowers to 'my dear Nellie'. The change took place in less than three years. It was easy for him to change, because his own allegiances, like those of his parents, were so mercurial, his own initial roots, unlike those of George Curzon or Harold Boulton, were so shallow, his own class identity and national identity so complex and easy to mould and manipulate.

By April 1881, when Gilbert and Sullivan's *Patience* was first performed in London, Oscar Wilde was well known enough for the character of Bunthorne, the Fleshy Poet, to be taken as a caricature of him. He had not yet published his first book of poems. He was famous for being famous even before he set out for America on 24 December 1881, and there he became even more famous. His sayings, and even things he did not say, were widely reported. He toured for one whole year there, giving 150 lectures and making six thousand dollars. He had three standard scripts: 'The Decorative Arts', 'The House Beautiful' and 'Irish Poets and Poetry of the Nineteenth Century'. 'Great success here,' he wrote to a friend,

> nothing like it since Dickens, they tell me. I am torn in bits by Society. Immense receptions, wonderful dinners, crowds wait for my carriage. I wave a gloved hand and an ivory cane and they cheer. Girls very lovely, men simple and intellectual. Rooms are hung with white lilies for me everywhere. I have 'Boy' [champagne] at intervals, also two secretaries, one to write my autograph and answer the hundreds of letters that come begging for it. Another, whose hair is brown, to send locks of his own hair to the young ladies who write asking for mine; he is rapidly becoming bald. Also a black servant, who is my slave – in a free country one cannot live without a slave – rather like a Christy Minstrel except he knows no riddles. Also a carriage and a black tiger [a black groom in livery] who is like a little monkey.

A month later, he wrote to another friend: 'I have a sort of triumphal progress, live like a young sybarite, travel like a young god.' He met Walt Whitman (who kissed him); he met Henry James (whom he insulted); he almost met Jesse James ('The Americans . . . always take their heroes from the criminal classes'); he had special clothes made ('The sleeves are to be flowered – if not velvet then plush-stamped with large pattern.

They will excite a great sensation.'); he met miners ('strong men wept like children' when he spoke of Botticelli); and Mormons ('very, very ugly'); and Indians ('Their conversation was most interesting as long as it was unintelligible.'). By May he was writing:

> I am now six feet high (my name on the placards), printed it is true in these primary colours against which I pass my life protesting, but still it is fame, and anything is better than virtuous obscurity.

Wilde arrived back in England on 6 January 1883 and then spent three months in Paris blowing the money he had made and meeting the famous writers and painters of the day. He then returned to London. On 26 November 1883, Constance Lloyd wrote to her brother Otho: 'Prepare yourself for an astounding piece of news! I am engaged to Oscar Wilde and perfectly and insanely happy.' Wilde wrote to Lillie Langtry:

> I am going to be married to a beautiful young girl called Constance Lloyd, a grave, slight, violet-eyed little Artemis, with great coils of heavy brown hair which make her flower-like head droop like a flower, and wonderful ivory hands which draw music from the piano so sweet that the birds stop singing to listen to her.

Between Wilde's marriage in May 1884 and the beginning of his friendship with Alfred Douglas eight years later, his letters display a mixture of domestic bliss and domestic unease, marital devotion and hints of what was to come. Early in December 1884, Wilde wrote a brief note to Philip Griffiths, a twenty-year-old from a wealthy family in Birmingham:

My dear, Philip, I have sent a photo of myself for you to the care of Mr MacKay which I hope you will like and in return for it you are to send me one of yourself which I shall keep as a memory of a charming meeting and golden hours passed together. You have a nature made to love all beautiful things and I hope we shall see each other soon.

A year later Wilde wrote to a friend:

Some day you will find, even as I have found, that there is no such thing as a romantic experience; there are romantic memories, and there is the desire of romance – that is all. Our most fiery moments of ecstasy are merely shadows of what somewhere else we have felt, or what we long some day to feel. So at least it seems to me. And, strangely enough, what comes of all this is a curious mixture of ardour and indifference. I myself would sacrifice everything for a new experience, and I know there is no such thing as a new experience at all.

By December 1888, he was thanking Robert Ross for the gift of a kitten. 'The children are enchanted with it, and sit, one on each side of the basket, worshipping.' Yeats in his *Autobiographies* wrote an account of a Christmas dinner Wilde invited him to, believing him to be alone in London.

> He had just renounced his velveteen, and even those cuffs turned backward over the sleeves, and had begun to dress very carefully in the fashion of the moment. He lived in a little house in Chelsea . . . I remember vaguely a white drawing-room with Whistler etchings, 'let in' to white panels, and a dining room all white, chairs, walls, mantelpiece, carpet, except for a diamond-shaped piece of red cloth in the middle of the table under a terra-cotta statuette, and I think a red-shaded lamp hanging from the ceiling to a little above the statuette . . . and I remember thinking that the perfect harmony of his life there, with his beautiful wife and his two young children, suggested some deliberate artistic composition . . . One form of success had gone: he was no more the lion of the season and he had not yet discovered his gift for writing comedy, yet I think I knew him at the happiest moment of his life.

In the summer of 1891, when he had already published *The Picture of Dorian Grey*, Wilde first met Alfred Douglas, who was twenty-one, but their friendship did not begin until the following year. In May or June 1892 Wilde wrote to Robert Ross:

> Bosie has insisted on stopping here for sandwiches. He is quite like a narcissus – so white and gold. I will

come either Wednesday or Thursday night to your rooms. Send me a line. Bosie is so tired: he lies like a hyacinth on the sofa, and I worship him.

By the following January, Wilde was writing to Douglas:

My own Boy, Your sonnet is quite lovely, and it is a marvel that those red rose-leaf lips of yours should have been made no less for music of song than for madness of kisses. Your slim gilt soul walks between passion and poetry. I know Hyacinthus, whom Apollo loved so madly, was you in Greek days.

By March the following year, Hyacinthus was making scenes:

Dearest of all Boys – Your letter was delightful – red and yellow wine to me – but I am sad and out of sorts – Bosie – you must not make scenes with me – they kill me – they wreck the loveliness of life – I cannot see *you*, so Greek and gracious, distorted by passion; I cannot listen to your curved lips saying hideous things to me – don't do it – you break my heart – I'd sooner be rented all day, than have you bitter, unjust, and horrid – horrid.

Thus the tone was set for the most famous gay relationship in history. The madness of kisses followed by the saying of hideous things; the distortion of passion. Oscar's forbearance and Douglas's bad temper both became famous; Oscar's generosity with money and Douglas's abuse of that generosity became the legend. 'Being kept was part of the pleasure of being loved,' Richard Ellmann wrote in his biography.

> Wilde's pleasure in the arrangement was perhaps a little less exquisite. Granted that he liked being abused a little, he could have foregone being abused so much. But Douglas enjoyed demanding ever higher flights of loving-kindness. When in 1894 his father threatened to cut off his allowance, Douglas encouraged him and threw himself upon Wilde's generosity. Since neither Wilde nor Douglas practised or expected sexual fidelity, money was the stamp and seal of their love.

That last sentence, so full of judgment and certainty, shows us perhaps more about Ellmann than it does about Wilde or Douglas. It suggests that 'since' they were not faithful to each other, they could not properly love each other; he suggests that 'since' this is the case, then the stamp and seal of their love would have to be something profane and abject and wrong.

It is much more likely that the stamp and seal of their love came from their enormous attraction to each other, their need for each other, and something difficult to define and explain which is at the core of homosexual experience in the era before gay liberation, and perhaps, to some extent, in the era afterwards.

In the letter quoted above about romantic experience, written after his marriage and five years before he met

Alfred Douglas, Wilde could write 'Our most fiery moments of ecstasy are merely shadows of what somewhere else we have felt, or of what we long some day to feel.' In most societies, most gay people go through adolescence believing that the fulfilment of physical desire would not be matched by emotional attachment. For straight people, the eventual matching of the two is part of the deal, a happy aspect of normality. But if this occurs for gay people, it is capable of taking on an extraordinarily powerful emotional force, and the resulting attachment, even if the physical part fizzles out, or even if the relationship makes no sense to the outside world, is likely to be fierce and enduring. The relationship between Auden and Chester Kallmann can be understood in this context, or the relationship between James Merrill and David Jackson. This, more likely, was the stamp and seal of the love between Oscar Wilde and Alfred Douglas.

In the years which followed their meeting we get two versions of Wilde's feelings for Douglas. In July 1894, he wrote:

> It is really absurd. I can't live without you. You are so dear, so wonderful. I think of you all day long, and miss your grace, your boyish beauty, the bright sword-play of your wit, the delicate fancy of your genius, so surprising always in its sudden swallow-flights towards north or south, towards sun or moon, and above all, you yourself . . . London is a desert without your dainty feet, and all the buttonholes have turned to weeds: nettles and hemlock are 'the only wear'.

In April 1895, from Holloway Prison, he wrote to
More Adey and Robert Ross: 'Bosie is so wonderful. I
think of nothing else. I saw him yesterday.' A week
later, he wrote: 'nothing but Alfred Douglas's daily
visits quicken me into life.' A few weeks later, he
wrote: 'Letter from Bosie, at Rouen, just arrived.
Please wire my thanks to him. He has cured me of sor-
row today.' On 15 May, Douglas wrote to Wilde from
Paris: 'It is too dreadful to be here without you' and
ended: 'I continue to think of you day and night, and
send you all my love. I am always your own loving
and devoted boy.'

In May 1895, when it was clear that Wilde was going
to go to prison, he wrote two last love letters to Alfred
Douglas:

> As for you, you have given me the beauty of life in the
> past, and in the future if there is any future . . . Never
> has anyone in my life been dearer than you, never has
> any love been greater, more sacred, more beautiful . . .
> the simple thought of you is enough to strengthen me
> and heal my wounds . . . Pain, if it comes, cannot last
> for ever; surely one day you and I will meet again, and
> though my face be a mask of grief and my body worn
> out by solitude, you and you alone will recognize the
> soul which is more beautiful for having met yours . . .
> Now I think of you as a golden-haired boy with
> Christ's own heart in you.

The second letter was written some days later. It
began: 'My child, Today it was asked to have the ver-

dicts rendered separately. Taylor [who was indicted with Wilde] is probably being judged at this moment, so that I have been able to come back here.' It ended:

> I decided it was nobler and more beautiful to stay [and face the trial]. We could not have been together. I did not want to be called a coward or a deserter. A false name, a disguise, a hunted life, all that is not for me, to whom you have been revealed on that high hill where beautiful things are transfigured. O sweetest of all boys, most loved of all loved, my soul clings to your soul, my life is your life, and in all the world of pain and pleasure, you are my ideal of admiration and joy.

Five days later, Wilde was sentenced to two years imprisonment with hard labour for 'acts of gross indecency'. There are no more letters for almost a year. And then, between January and March 1897, Wilde worked on a long letter to Douglas, later known as 'De Profundis', from Reading Jail, the governor having given permission for the pages to be taken away each night and brought back in the morning. On his release he gave it to Robert Ross, who gave a copy to Douglas, who would claim that he never received it. Although it appeared in various versions after Wilde's death, the complete text was not published until 1949.

The tone of 'De Profundis' was calmly eloquent; there was a hurt beauty in the sentences, and a sense of urgency, a sense of hard things being said for the first time. Wilde's old skills at paradox, his ability to use words as a way of turning the world on its head, were no longer used to seduce an audience but to kill his own pain and grief. He was ready to accuse, who was once so ready to praise and flatter. He had suffered too much to care if his tone seemed too emotional, written not as art, but as matter. 'If there be in it one single passage that brings tears to your eyes, weep as we weep in prison where the day no less than the night is set apart for tears.' Suddenly, in what is perhaps the most shocking sentence in the whole long letter, Wilde was able to write: 'The supreme vice is shallowness.'

He accused Douglas of distracting him from his art, of spending his money, of degrading him ethically, of constant scene-making, of deliberately mistreating him and then of thoughtlessly mistreating him. He blamed Douglas for his ruin. He went over Douglas's bad behaviour, sometimes citing dates and places and details, but managing throughout to hold a tone which was fluent, to write a prose of sweeping cadences and measured elegance, to create a voice both indignant and controlled.

> Had our life together been as the world fancied it to be, one simply of pleasure, profligacy and laughter, I would not be able to recall a single passage in it. It is because it was full of moments and days, tragic, bitter, sinister in their warnings, dull and dreadful in their monotonous scenes and unseemly violences, that I can see or hear each separate incident in its detail, can indeed see or hear little else.

Some of his cry from the depths was so sad that it would make you want to burst with laughter. He recalled Douglas's fever while staying at that well-known Irish haunt, the Grand Hotel in Brighton:

> Except for an hour's walk in the morning, an hour's drive in the afternoon, I never left the hotel. I got special grapes from London for you, as you did not care for those the hotel supplied, invented things to please you, remained either with you or in the room next to yours, sat with you every evening to quiet and amuse you.

Soon afterwards, when Wilde himself fell ill,

> the next two days you leave me entirely alone without care, without attendance, without anything. It was not a question of grapes, flowers and charming gifts: it was a question of mere necessaries: I could not even get the milk the doctor had ordered for me.

'Of course,' he wrote, 'I should have got rid of you.' Instead,

> through deep if misplaced affection for you: through great pity for your defects of temper and temperament: through my own proverbial good nature and Celtic laziness: through an artistic aversion to coarse scenes and ugly words . . . I gave up to you always.

But he did not answer the question which every forlorn phrase of 'De Profundis' begged: why did he *not* get rid of Douglas, walk away from him, grapes and all? Since Wilde's good nature and his Celtic laziness, not to speak of his pity and his artistic aversion, did not cause him to remain with Constance Lloyd, what made him stay with Douglas? In 'De Profundis', he wrote about love.

> You loved me far better than you loved anybody else. But you, like myself, have had a terrible tragedy in your life . . . Do you want to learn what it was? It was this. In you Hate was always stronger than Love.

Why did it take two years hard labour for him to realise this? Why did he not put an end to what Richard Ellmann calls his 'berserk passion' much earlier? In Wilde's 'De Profundis', the love that dared not speak its name was not the love of domesticity, or mutual kindness and respect, it was love in a dark time, in what Ellmann called 'a clandestine world of partial disclosures, blackmail, and libel suits'. The emotions around the time when Wilde and Douglas discovered one another, and found happiness with each other, were not recounted or recalled, they remain private and undocumented. This love between Wilde and Douglas, their fierce attachment, formed the basis for every decision made. And the emotion arising from those nights they first spent with each other, which does not speak its name much in 'De Profundis', made him and Douglas, despite all the treachery and all the badness, inseparable.

'The only beautiful things,' Vivian told us in 'The Decay of Lying' (1890), 'are the things that do not concern us. As long as a thing is useful or necessary to us, or affects us in any way, either for pain or for pleasure, or appeals strongly to our sympathies, or is a vital part of the environment in which we live, it is outside the proper sphere of art.' Vivian, in this dialogue with Cyril (Wilde gave his sons' names to the characters), dismissed all the contemporary novelists in English.

> Mr Henry James writes fiction as if it were a painful duty, and wastes upon mean motives and imperceptible 'points of view' his neat literary style, his felicitous phrases, his swift and caustic satire.

Vivian went on to praise Balzac: 'He created life, he did not copy it.' And later Vivian expounded the view that Life is thin and pale while Art is strong and bright and Life thus reflects and follows Art.

> Schopenhauer has analysed the pessimism that characterizes modern thought, but Hamlet invented it. The world has become sad because a puppet was once melancholy.

Yeats had his doubts about that last sentence.

> I said: 'Why do you change "sad" to "melancholy"?' He replied that he wanted a full sound at the close of his sentence, and I thought it no excuse and an example

of the vague impressiveness that spoiled his writing
for me.

But surely Yeats was wrong; surely the sentence is
perfectly managed. 'Sad' cannot be repeated; it is, in
any case, a more definite word than 'melancholy', so
that it suggests that the mere melancholy of the actor
made the world something harder and more intense
than melancholy. And because melancholy has four
syllables and sad just one, and because of the sound
those four syllables make, there is something open
and suggestive about the word placed at the end of
the sentence, a word which could have influence,
rather than a word that stops dead. There are times
in the plays and the letters and the prose works when
Wilde seems to have the most exquisite ear for what
a sentence can do. He loved the ring and balance of
an English sentence.

What was missing from his poetry until 'The Ballad
of Reading Gaol' (1898) was this voice of his. Every
word he wrote in prose, or in the four plays *Lady
Windermere's Fan*, *A Woman of No Importance*, *An
Ideal Husband* and *The Importance of Being Earnest*
was knowing and sharply precise. His language not
only protected itself from the reader's irony, but took
full responsibility for the irony and demanded more.
The poems, on the other hand, seemed to be waiting
to be mocked and parodied. Nonetheless, he cared
about them, and sent them to editor after editor.
Between 1877 and 1881, when his first volume of
poems appeared, he published, according to Ian Small,

'some forty poems in Irish, American and English periodicals'.

Just as the sombre, urgent tone of 'De Profundis' was light years from the flippant and amusing tone of 'The Decay of Lying', just as the former was forced to break the rules which the latter had established, 'The Ballad of Reading Gaol' did everything the earlier poetry refused to do. 'The only beautiful things are the things that do not concern us.' Wilde discovered desperately that no aspect of this sentence was true. For good reasons, he ceased to care about beautiful things and he developed a serious need to deal precisely with what concerned him. And since 'De Profundis' was his best prose and 'The Ballad of Reading Gaol' his best poetry, the story of his downfall is not interesting simply for its own drama but for what it did to him as an artist, how it forced him to abandon everything he believed in to find a new tone. 'Mad Ireland hurt you into poetry,' Auden wrote about Yeats. For Wilde, two years in prison and disgrace hurt him into a new style, direct and confessional, serious and emotional. His words now were arrows rather than feathers. He retained, however, aspects of the genius he declared when he first passed through customs in America: a sense of shape and form, an ability to create memorable phrases. He knew how to harness his old skills so that he could haunt the world with the experience had been through.

He wrote no plays after being in prison. His four best plays, written between 1891 and 1894, express his spirit at its most free, ready to mock and amuse, use old creaky plots and old creaky characters, and use them to play with a world of surfaces and secrets. Mistaken identities, long-lost children, lost jewels, overheard conversations and many exits and entrances are placed beside cynicism and corruption, opportunism and a large number of aphorisms which manage to seem both glib and indisputable. ('Morality is simply the attitude we adopt towards people whom we personally dislike.' 'Scandal is gossip made tedious by morality.' 'The youth of the present day are quite monstrous. They have absolutely no respect for dyed hair.')

These plays seem to have been written effortlessly and this, most of the time, is unfortunate: they needed more effort. *Lady Windermere's Fan*, *A Woman of No Importance* and *An Ideal Husband* depend too much on the jokes; the plotting is often clunky and the tying up of the plot seems lazy and mechanical like bad French farces. Wilde was not talented at creating character, and in these years he would, in any case, have despised the idea. This did not prevent him carefully considering other writers' characters. It is interesting how close the character of Mrs Erlynne in *Lady Windermere's Fan*, for example, is to Madame Merle in *The Portrait of a Lady* ('oh so flat "fizz",' James wrote of the play in 1911), or how close the character of Hester in *A Woman of No Importance* is to many of James's heroines, or how close Lady Bracknell is to Lady Catherine de Burgh.

It is important to remember that these plays were written by an Irish nationalist living in London in the few years after the fall of Parnell (who died in 1891) when two of the most virulent strains of hypocrisy ever known – English hypocrisy and Irish hypocrisy – joined forces for the first and only time in history. Wilde had been a supporter of Parnell and had attended meetings of the Parnell Commission in the late 1880s when the leader was accused of collusion with political violence. *An Ideal Husband* placed at its centre a story of corruption in the British Cabinet. Wilde's last play, however, his most perfect work, did something more powerful and subtle. It dealt with two subjects about which he had strong and complex feelings in 1894 – England and marriage. It mattered enormously to him that both should fall into decay. His play was set among an idle and cynical English ruling-class, and it is a play about love and marriage where love is governed by whim and marriage is mercenary. His genius in *The Importance of Being Earnest* was to make all this seem obvious, so deeply built into the fabric of the play that the audience would not notice it. They would notice instead the jokes and the perfect patterning, every piece of action mirrored, the development of the plot ingenious and perfect. The audience would not notice the poisoned arrows buried in the feathers.

The problem about all Wilde's work, but his plays especially, is that they are forced to compete with the drama of his own last years. There are lines in the plays which seem haunted now by the story of the life. In *The Importance of Being Earnest*, when Jack says that his brother 'expressed a desire to be buried

in Paris', Dr Chasuble replies: 'In Paris! (Shakes his
head.) I fear that hardly points to any great state
of mind at the last.' Later, Gwendolyn says: 'And
certainly once a man begins to neglect his domestic
duties he becomes painfully effeminate.' And since
Wilde's greatest public humiliation occurred, as he
recounted in 'De Profundis', on a railway station
where he was jeered by a crowd while being taken
from one prison to another, Lady Bracknell's line:
'Come, my dear, we have already missed five, if not
six, trains. To miss more might expose us to comment
on the platform' can affect the audience in a way
that Wilde never dreamed of. Also, in both *Lady
Windermere's Fan* and *A Woman of No Importance*,
the issue of morality and forgiveness is rehearsed.
In *An Ideal Husband* Lady Chiltern says that life 'has
taught me that a person who has once been guilty
of a dishonourable action may be guilty of it a second
time, and should be shunned.' When Lady Windermere is asked if she thinks that 'women who have
committed what the world calls a fault should never
be forgiven,' she says: 'I think they should never be
forgiven.' 'And men?' she is asked. 'Do you think that
there should be the same laws for men as there are for
women?' 'Certainly!' she replies. And then: 'If we had
these "hard and fast rules", we should find life much
more simple.'

In November 1895 Henry James refused to sign a
petition for mitigation of Wilde's sentence. Through

his friend Jonathan Sturges, he made clear that 'the petition would not have the slightest effect on the authorities here . . . and that the document would only exist as a manifesto of personal loyalty to Oscar by his friends, of which he [James] was never one'. In his biography, Richard Ellmann wrote: 'People not familiar with prisons had no idea what their procedures were. That is perhaps the only excuse for Henry James, who wrote to Paul Bourget that Wilde's sentence to hard labour was too severe, that isolation would have been more just.'

Close to Wilde's release date, the governor of Reading Gaol said to Robert Ross: 'He looks well. But like all men unused to manual labour who receive a sentence of this kind, he will be dead within two years.' Wilde could not sleep on the board provided; he could not eat the food and suffered from dreadful diarrhoea. He was alone for twenty-three hours a day, and was not allowed to speak during the hour of exercise. For most of the time he had no writing paper, and was allowed two books a week from the library, but the library was useless. He had problems with his ears and his eyes. He had to work at picking oakum, or at the treadmill. Letters and visits were strictly limited. He and his friends made various efforts to have his sentence commuted, but he served two years to the day. In October 1895, five months into his sentence, Arthur Clifton, whom Wilde wanted to become guardian of his children, visited him: 'He looked dreadfully thin. You can imagine how painful it was to meet him: and he was very much upset and cried a good deal: he seemed quite broken-hearted and kept on describing his punishment as savage . . . He was terribly despondent and said several times that he did not think that he would be able to see the punishment out.'

On his release he wrote several letters to the *Daily Chronicle* about his time in prison.

> On Saturday week last I was in my cell at about one o'clock occupied in cleaning and polishing the tins I had been using for dinner. Suddenly I was startled by the prison silence being broken by the most horrible and revolting shrieks, or rather howls, for at first I thought some animals like a bull or a cow was being unskillfully slaughtered outside the prison walls. I soon realized, however, that the howls proceeded from the basement of the prison, and I knew that some wretched man was being flogged . . . The next day . . . I saw the poor fellow at exercise, his weak, ugly, wretched face bloated by tears and hysteria almost beyond recognition . . . He was a living grotesque. The other prisoners all watched him, and not one of them smiled. Everybody knew what had happened to him, and that he was being driven insane – was insane already.

After his release he wrote to and tried to help several of his fellow inmates. In a letter to a friend, he explained that

> you must understand that I have the deepest desire to try and be of a little help to other fellows who were

in trouble with me. I used to be utterly reckless of young lives: I used to take up a boy, love him 'passionately' and then grow bored with him, and often take no notice of him. That is what I regret in my past life. Now I feel that if I can really help others it will be a little attempt, however small, at expiation.

In March 1898, less than a year after his release, as reform of the prison system was being debated – and reforms were implemented later that year – he wrote to the *Daily Chronicle* once more.

There are three permanent punishments authorized by law in English prisons. 1. Hunger 2. Insomnia 3. Disease . . . Every prisoner suffers day and night from hunger . . . The result of the food – which in most cases consists of weak gruel, badly-baked bread, suet and water – is disease in the form of incessant diarrhoea . . . With regard to the punishment of insomnia, it only exists in Chinese and English prisons. In China it is inflicted by placing the prisoner in a small bamboo cage; in England by means of the plank bed. The object of the plank bed is to produce insomnia. There is no other object in it, and it invariably succeeds . . . Deprived of books, of all human intercourse, isolated from every humane and humanising influence, condemned to eternal silence, robbed of all intercourse with the external world, treated like an unintelligent animal, brutalized below the level of any of the brute-creation, the wretched man who is confined in an English prison can hardly escape becoming insane.

In the months after his release Wilde had trouble convincing those around him that he had been broken by his experiences. In June, three weeks after his release, he wrote to Frank Harris:

> You must try to realize what two years' cellular confinement is, and what two years of absolute silence means to a man of my intellectual powers . . . When he [the prisoner] goes out, he finds he has still to suffer. His punishment, as far as its effects go, lasts intellectually and physically, just as it lasts socially.

In February 1898, he wrote again to Harris, who had suggested that he write another play:

> As regards a comedy . . . I have lost the mainspring of life and art, la joie de vivre; it is dreadful. I have pleasures, and passions, but the joy of life is gone. I am going under: the morgue yawns for me.

'The intense energy of creation has been kicked out of me,' he wrote to another friend in August 1897. A year later he wrote to Ross:

> I don't think I shall ever write again. Something is killed in me. I feel no desire to write. I am unconscious of power. Of course, my first year in prison destroyed me body and soul.

After his release, he went to France and worked on 'The Ballad of Reading Gaol' and tried to deal with the two people whom he had most loved – Constance and Alfred Douglas – as they tried to deal with him. In 'De Profundis', Wilde wrote about his mother's death while he was in prison:

> I had disgraced that name eternally. I had made it a low byword among low people . . . My wife, at that time kind and gentle to me, rather than that I should hear the news from indifferent or alien lips, travelled, ill as she was, all the way from Geneva to London to break to me herself the tidings of so irreparable, so irredeemable a loss . . . You [Douglas] alone stood aloof, sent me no message, and wrote me no letter.

Wilde, early in his prison sentence, was declared a bankrupt and his possessions were sold, including the rights to his plays. His mother had been buried in a pauper's grave. Constance had left England and changed her name to Holland. In the vast correspondence between all the main players in the life of Oscar Wilde, a short letter from Constance, written to a fortune teller in April 1895, is perhaps the most telling and poignant.

> My dear Mrs Robinson, What is to become of my husband who has so betrayed and deceived me and ruined the lives of my darling boys? Can you tell me anything? You told me that after this terrible shock my life was to become easier, but will there be any

happiness in it, or is that dead for me? And I have had so little. My life has all been cut to pieces as my hand is by its lines.

Constance had money, and Robert Ross arranged with her that Wilde should have an allowance. The details of this arrangement caused Wilde much grief in his last days in prison. In short, he believed that it was not enough and that there were too many strings attached. One of these strings was that she could withdraw his allowance if he created a scandal or spent time with disreputable people, i.e. if he returned to Douglas. And Douglas, who believed that he had suffered just as much as Wilde, wanted to return to him. On 4 June 1897, Wilde wrote to him from the Hotel de la Plage, Berneval-sur-Mer: 'Don't think I don't love you. Of course I love you more than anyone else. But our lives are irreparably severed as far as meeting goes.' However, on 15 June he wrote again: 'You ask me to let you come on Saturday: but dear honey-sweet boy, I have already asked you to come then: so we both have the same desire, as usual.' He suggested that Douglas use the name Jonquil du Vallon, as he was using the name Sebastian Melmoth. (Charles Maturin, who wrote *Melmoth the Wanderer*, was Wilde's grand-uncle.) Two days later he changed his mind again: 'Of course at present it is impossible for us to meet . . . Later on, when the alarm in England is over, when secrecy is possible, and silence forms part of the world's attitude, we may meet, but at present you see it is impossible.' On 24 August, Wilde wrote to

Robert Ross: 'Since Bosie wrote that he could not afford forty francs to come to Rouen to see me, he has never written. Nor have I. I am greatly hurt by his meanness and lack of imagination.' A week later, Wilde wrote to Douglas:

> My own Darling Boy, I got your telegram half an hour ago, and just sent you a line to say that my only hope of again doing beautiful work in art is being with you . . . Everyone is furious with me for going back to you, but they don't understand us . . . Do remake my ruined life for me, and then our friendship and love will have a different meaning to the world.

Three weeks later, from Naples where he had gone with Douglas, he tried to explain what he had done to Robert Ross: 'When people speak against me for going back to Bosie, tell them that he offered me love, and that in my loneliness and disgrace I, after three months' struggle against a hideous Philistine world, turned naturally to him.' He wrote many letters defending himself, including a letter to his publisher Leonard Smithers:

> [Douglas] is witty, graceful, lovely to look at, love-able to be with. He has also ruined my life, so I can't help loving him – it is the only thing to do. My wife's letter came too late. I had waited four months in vain, and it was only when the children had gone back to school that she asked me to come to her – whereas what I want is the love of my children. It is

now irretrievable, of course. But in questions of the emotions and their romantic qualities, unpunctuality is fatal.

Wilde and Douglas moved in these months from being an interchangeable Frankenstein and the monster to becoming Romeo and Juliet. Among those who wanted to break up their relationship and put an end to them setting up house in Naples were Douglas's mother, who controlled his income, Douglas's father, who still could not control his rage, and Constance, who believed that Wilde had sacrificed himself because of Douglas's irrational hatred for his father. In early October Wilde wrote to Robert Ross.

I am awaiting a thunderbolt from my wife's solicitor. She wrote me a terrible letter, but a foolish one, saying 'I *forbid you*' to do so and so: 'I will not *allow* you' etc: and 'I *require* a distinct promise that you will not' etc. How can she really imagine that she can influence or control my life? She might just as well try to influence and control my art . . . So I suppose she will now try to deprive me of my wretched £3 a week. Women are so petty, and Constance has no imagination.

Constance wrote to her friend, Carlos Blacker:

I have today written a note to Oscar saying that I required an immediate answer to my question whether he had been to Capri or whether he had met anywhere that appalling individual. I also said that he evidently did not care much for his boys since he neither acknowledged their photos which I sent him nor the remembrances *they* sent him. I hope it was not too hard of me to write this, but it was quite necessary.

Wilde remained unrepentant. On 16 November, he wrote to Ross:

My existence is a scandal. But I do not think I should be charged with creating a scandal by continuing to live: though I am conscious that I do so. I cannot live alone, and Bosie is the only one of my friends who is either able or willing to give me his companionship.

Two days later Constance wrote to her brother:

I have stopped O's allowance as he is living with Lord Alfred Douglas, so in a short time war will be declared! His legal friends in London make no defence and so far make no opposition, as it was always understood that if he went back to that person his allowance would stop.

Wilde was indignant:

I did not think that on my release my wife, my trustees, the guardians of my children, my few friends, such as they are, and my myriad enemies would combine to force me by starvation to live in silence and solitude again.

As the arguments went back and forth about his relationship with Douglas, Wilde wrote a long letter to his publisher about the design of 'The Ballad of Reading Gaol' and the wording of the dedication. Wilde believed, he said, that dedicating the poem to R.J.M. would be enough and then he added:

> Alfred Douglas thinks that if I don't put that R.J.M. died in Reading Prison people might think that it was all imaginary. This is a sound objection.

These two sentences are significant, because they are the only time we get Douglas in these years (or indeed any years) not screaming, or complaining, or causing grief, or not being madly loved. This is a brief glimpse of ordinary life between Wilde and Douglas, discussing something of interest to Wilde which Douglas, who also published poetry, knew something about.

By February they had split up and Wilde was in Paris. On 4 March, Constance wrote to Carlos Blacker:

> Oscar is or at least was at the Hotel de Nice, rue des Beaux-Arts . . . He has, as you know, behaved exceedingly badly both to myself and my children and all possibility of our living together has come to an end . . . if you do see him tell him that I think 'The Ballad' exquisite, and I hope that the great success it has had in London at all events will urge him on to write more. I hear that he does nothing now but

drink and I heard that he had left Lord A. and had received £200 from Lady Q. on condition that he did not see him again, but of course, this may be untrue. Is Lord A. in Paris?

Constance was well-informed. Wilde had, in fact, received £200 from Lady Queensberry, and it was true that he did nothing in Paris but drink. But Lord A. was not in Paris. 'I have a sort of idea she [Constance] really wants me to be dead,' Wilde wrote to Carlos Blacker to whom Constance also wrote:

Oscar is so pathetic and such a born actor, and I am hardened when I am away from him. No words will describe my horror of that BEAST, for I will call him nothing else A.D. . . . I do not wish him [Oscar] dead, but . . . I think he might leave his wife and children alone.

Soon, Wilde began to think over what had happened between himself and Douglas in Naples and wrote to Ross: 'I know it is better that I should never see him again. I don't want to. He fills me with horror.'

Constance died in April at the age of forty. Wilde wrote to Harris: 'My way back to hope and a new life ends in her grave.' But when Robert Ross came to visit he noted that 'Oscar of course does not feel it at all.' Wilde had no access to the children, and he never saw them again. He was granted £150 a year from Constance's estate. 'He really did not understand how cruel he was to his wife,' Robert Ross wrote after his death. In Paris he began to see Douglas again, but the meetings were sporadic and difficult.

Many of the letters from his last three years are about money. He was always waiting for money, writing for money and running out of money. He was petulant and knew how to complain. But there are also brilliant passages, worthy of him in the old days, but with a new anger and edge:

> I never came across anyone in whom the moral sense was dominant who was not heartless, cruel, vindictive, log-stupid and entirely lacking in the smallest sense of humanity. Moral people, as they are termed, are simple beasts. I would sooner have fifty unnatural vices than one unnatural virtue. It is unnatural virtue that makes the world, for those who suffer, such a premature Hell.

He continued, or so he said, his unnatural vices, writing to Ross from Rome in April 1900 about a young seminarian he had befriended:

> I also gave him many *lire*, and prophesied for him a Cardinal's hat, if he remained very good, and never forgot me. He said he never would, and indeed I don't think he will, for every day I kissed him behind the high altar.

Five days later he had more news:

> I have given up Armando, a very smart elegant young Roman Sporus. He was beautiful, but his request for

raiment and neckties were incessant: he really bayed for boots, as a dog moonwards.

In October 1900, Wilde became ill. In late November, Robert Ross, who later wrote that he had always promised to bring a priest to Wilde when he was dying, came to Paris and found a priest who baptised Wilde into the Catholic Church and gave him the last rites. As Wilde lay dying in his hotel room, Ross and Reginald Turner 'destroyed letters to keep ourselves from breaking down.' Douglas came to Paris for the funeral. He himself was to live until 1945.

Wilde was buried first at Bagneaux outside Paris in a cheap grave, but in 1909 he was re-buried in Père Lachaise with a beautiful sculpture by Jacob Epstein as his gravestone. Robert Ross's ashes were interred there when he died in 1918. In 1899 Wilde had written to Ross about his visit to Constance's grave in Genoa:

> It is very pretty – a marble cross with dark ivy-leaves inlaid in a good pattern. The cemetery is a garden at the foot of the lovely hills that climb into the mountains that girdle Genoa. It was very tragic seeing her name carved on a tomb – her surname, my name not mentioned of course.

In 1963, the words 'Wife of Oscar Wilde' were carved on the headstone. A memorial to Lady Wilde was incorporated into the family grave in Mount Jerome in Dublin in 1996 and a headstone erected over her grave in Kensal Green in 2000. In 1995, Oscar Wilde was included in a window in Westminster Abbey. As the centenary of his death approached, statues to commemorate him were erected in Dublin and London.

The personal became political because an Irishman in London pushed his luck. He remains a vivid presence in the world one hundred years after his death. He played out the role of the tragic queer. He was witty, the greatest talker of his generation, skilled in the art of the one-liner, the quick aside. But he was also untrustworthy and he was doomed. He was Faust, who stole some years of pleasure and fame, to be rewarded with the plank bed, the treadmill and an early death. He was also an Irish nationalist and socialist wandering among the rich and powerful in London salons, eventually being punished for his cheek. His letters show how ambitious he was, and pompous, and how funny he also was, a lord of language as he said himself, and how savagely he was destroyed by his two years in prison. He invented self-invention. He was pure fin-de-siècle in his tone and manners until his tone and manners were forced to change. A few times in his short life he created works which were either brilliant ideas, or masterpieces of tone and cadence, or formally flawless.

In the summer of 1947, André Gide, shortly before he was awarded the Nobel Prize and four years before his death, went to Oxford to receive an honorary doctorate. Part of his reason for going there was to visit Oscar Wilde's rooms in Magdalen College. Gide had signed the clemency petition in 1895 and, after

Wilde's release, had gone to visit him at Berneval on the French coast. In Wilde's last years in Paris, however, Gide had seen him only twice. Although he had given him money, he had been embarrassed by him, by his seediness and his reputation for consorting with local rent boys. Gide, despite everything, had become respectable. At his first meeting, he tried to sit opposite Wilde with his back to the street so no one would see him. Now he walked into the rooms where Wilde had begun the transformation of himself. He stood and looked around as an undergraduate cricket team, who were having a party in the room, fell silent. He paid no attention to them; he ran the fingers of one hand along the wall, saying nothing, trying to conjure up the fearless presence who had guessed the truth about him and changed his life more than fifty years before.

The Complete Letters of Oscar Wilde edited by Merlin Holland and Rupert Hart-Davis, Fourth Estate

The Complete Works of Oscar Wilde: Volume I: Poems and Poems in Prose edited by Bobby Fong and Karl Beckson, OUP

ROGER CASEMENT:

SEX, LIES AND THE BLACK DIARIES

JESSIE CONRAD REMEMBERED HIS VISIT:

> Sir Roger Casement, a fanatical Irish protestant, came
> to see us, remaining some two days our guest. He was
> a very handsome man with a thick, dark beard and
> piercing, restless eyes. His personality impressed me
> greatly. It was about the time when he was interested
> in bringing to light certain atrocities which were tak-
> ing place in the Belgian Congo. Who could foresee his
> own terrible fate during the war as he stood in our
> drawing room passionately denouncing the cruelties
> he had seen?

One of Conrad's biographers, Frederick Karl, is
unsure when this visit took place, but if we are to
believe Casement's Black Diary – and Angus Mitchell,
who has edited *The Amazon Journal of Roger
Casement*, thinks that we should not – it took place
on 3 January 1904 and lasted only one day.

Joseph Conrad had met Casement first in 1889 or
1890 in the Congo, when Casement was working for

the Congo Railway Company. 'For some three weeks,' Conrad wrote,

> he lived in the same room in the Matadi Station of the Belgian Société du Haut-Congo. He was rather reticent as to the exact character of his connection with it; but the work he was busy about then was recruiting labour. He knew the coast languages well. I went with him several times on short expeditions to hold 'palavers' with neighbouring village chiefs. The object of them was recruiting porters for the Company's caravans from Matadi to Leopoldville – or rather to Kinchassa (on Stanley Pool). Then I went up into the interior to take up my command of the stern-wheeler 'Roi des Belges' and he, apparently, remained on the coast.

The visit which was remembered by Jessie Conrad had a purpose. Casement had read *Heart of Darkness* and he wanted Conrad to support him in the case he was making against atrocities in the Congo. 'I am glad you read the Heart of D. tho' of course it's an awful fudge,' Conrad had written to him. Conrad had based *Heart of Darkness* on his impressions – he had very little hard, detailed evidence – but, in any case, he did not want to get involved. He wrote to his friend R.B. Cunninghame Graham:

> He is a Protestant Irishman, pious too. But so was Pizarro. For the rest I can assure you that he is a limpid personality. There is a touch of the conquistador

in him too; for I have seen him start off into an unspeakable wilderness swinging a crookhandled stick for all weapon with two bull-dogs, Paddy (white) and Biddy (brindle) at his heels and a Loanda boy carrying a bundle for company. A few months afterwards it so happened that I saw him come out again, a little leaner, a little browner, with his stick dogs and Loanda boy, and quietly serene as though he had been for a stroll in the park. He . . . lately seems to have been sent to the Congo on some sort of mission by the British government. I always thought some particle of Las Casas' soul had found refuge in his indomitable body . . . I would help him but it is not in me. I am only a wretched novelist inventing wretched stories, and not even up to that miserable game . . . He could tell you things! Things I have tried to forget, things I never did know. He had as many years of Africa as I had months – almost.

After Casement's arrest in 1916, Conrad wrote to John Quinn in New York:

We never talked politics . . . He was a good companion: but already in Africa I judged that he was a man, properly speaking, of no mind at all. I don't mean stupid. I meant that he was all emotion. By emotional force (Congo report, Putumayo etc) he made his way, and sheer emotionalism has undone him. A creature of sheer temperament – a truly tragic personality: all but the greatness of which he had not a trace. Only vanity. But in the Congo it was not visible yet.

Roger Casement was born in Ireland in 1864, of a prosperous Protestant family. He was brought up mainly in Northern Ireland. At the age of twenty he went to Africa, where he worked with various commercial interests in the Congo and then in what later became Nigeria. Subsequently, he found employment with the British Consular Service and in 1900 returned to the Congo, part of which was under the direct control of Leopold II, King of the Belgians. He began to investigate allegations of brutality in the region; his work was thorough and conscientious, and he was personally responsible for the decision of the Foreign Office to undertake a serious investigation of what was happening in the Congo.

In 1906 Casement began to work in the British Consular Service in South America: in Santos, Rio de Janeiro and then in Pará at the mouth of the Amazon. In 1910 he investigated allegations of atrocities against the Amazon Indians. He was knighted for his work. By the time he resigned from the Consular Service in 1913, he had become a fervent Irish nationalist; and on his return to Ireland he was made treasurer of the Irish Volunteers. He was a glittering prize for the new movement: a Protestant, a knight, an internationally-known humanitarian and anti-imperialist. He worked for the Irish cause in the United States and Germany, raising funds in the United States and trying to start an Irish Brigade with prisoners of war in Germany. He landed from Germany, after much adventure, on the coast of county Kerry on Good Friday 1916 in a German submarine, but the guns which were to come as well failed to arrive. He was captured and taken to London, where he was charged with treason. He was found guilty. His diaries, in particular his 'Black' Diaries – which consisted of diaries for 1903, 1910, 1911 and a ledger for 1911, and gave accounts of homosexual encounters in Africa and South America – were used to prevent a reprieve. He was hanged. After his death, there was great controversy about the diaries. Were they forged? Were they real? How could an Irish patriot be homosexual? Many books have been published on the subject. In 1996 two new books were published which dealt with Casement's legacy: one of them believed that the diaries were genuine, the other did not.

Casement's bones, or what was left of them – he had been buried without a coffin in quicklime – were returned to Ireland by Harold Wilson's government in February 1965. The first request had been made to Ramsay MacDonald's government sometime between 1929 and 1931. This was refused, as were de Valera's requests to Stanley Baldwin and Churchill, and Sean Lemass's request to Harold Macmillan. In her account of the discussions between the two governments about Casement's body, and indeed Casement's diaries, in the spring 1996 edition of *Irish Archives*, from which this information was taken, Deirdre McMahon writes:

Exasperated British ministers and officials were apt to attribute malice to de Valera's concern for Casement:

but in fact the controversy revealed the cultural chasm in Irish and British attitudes to death. What to the Irish was respect for the dead, to the British was a distasteful and morbid obsession.

The exhumation took place after dark in Pentonville Prison: Casement had not been buried, as had been believed, beside Dr Crippen, according to the documents which the British officials had, but between two men called Kuhn and Robinson. The lower jaw, eight ribs, several vertebrae, arm bones, shoulder bones, a number of smaller bones and the skull, virtually intact and still covered with bits of the shroud, were found and put into a coffin. The bones belonged to a man of exceptional height – Casement was tall. The British paid for the coffin. ('It was a gesture which they felt they should make and were glad to make,' an Irish official said.) There was a state funeral in Dublin. The coffin was buried in Glasnevin Cemetery beside others who had fought and suffered for the cause of Ireland: Daniel O'Connell, Charles Stewart Parnell, Paddy Dignam.

Although there is a large collection of Casement documents in the National Library in Dublin (and other items which he brought back from Africa and South America – including costumes and a butterfly collection – in the National Museum and the Natural History Museum), his diaries remain in England. They were seen by Michael Collins and Eamon Duggan during the 1921 Treaty negotiations. In the early Thirties Duggan wrote:

Michael Collins and I saw the Casement Diary by arrangement with Lord Birkenhead. We read it. I did not know Casement's handwriting. Collins did. He said it was his. The diary was in two parts – bound volumes – repeating ad nauseam details of sex perversion – of the personal appearance and beauty of native boys – with special reference to a certain portion of their anatomy. It was disgusting.

De Valera was careful not to become involved in the controversy about the diaries which erupted at regular intervals during his time in office, and he refused to ask the British Government to allow his representative to check their authenticity. When the diaries were published in Paris and New York in 1959, a British official asked a diplomat at the Irish Embassy in London what the reaction in Ireland would be to the release of the diaries, adding that 'in view of the present attitude in Britain to homosexuality, few people now in this country would attach much importance to Casement's failings in this respect.' The Irish diplomat had to reveal that here perhaps was another cultural chasm between Ireland and Britain: 'Opinion in Ireland had not moved so far and would probably not be much different from what it was in this country when Casement was on trial.'

When Sean Lemass came to power in 1959, he was anxious to have the diaries as well as the body, and the Irish Cabinet agreed that the diaries should be given to the Irish Government, with no copy being kept by the British, but Maurice Moynihan, secretary to the

Government and secretary to the Department of the Taoiseach, was against this. Did the Government intend to keep them, to burn them, to publish them, he asked. In his opinion, the Irish Government should have nothing to do with them. Lemass eventually agreed with him. On 23 July, R.A. Butler announced that the diaries would be deposited in the Public Record Office in London, where they could be viewed by scholars and historians. Southern Ireland wanted Casement's bones since they held no secrets and could not speak, but the diaries were, and still are, dynamite, and the English, as we all know, are better at handling that sort of thing.

The Black Diaries first became available in 1959. *The Black Diaries: An Account of Roger Casement's Life and Times, with a Collection of His Diaries and Public Writings*, by Peter Singleton-Gates and Maurice Girodias, published by Grove Press in New York and the Olympia Press in Paris, was an extraordinary book. It included potted histories of Ireland, the Congo and the Putumayo in the Amazon basin, an account of Casement's life and death, his report on the Congo, his report on the Putumayo, his diary from the Congo in 1903 and his diary from the Putumayo in 1910. The diary entries were placed facing the reports, so that on the left-hand page you got clear, factual statements about brutality, and accounts of Casement's investigations often laced with his indignation, and on the right-hand page you got cryptic notes, times, money spent, meetings registered, the weather, news, opinions. On 17 April 1903 he noted Sir Hector Macdonald's suicide in Paris – Macdonald was charged with homosexual activities in Ceylon – and wrote: 'The reasons given are pitiably sad. The most distressing case this surely of its kind and one that may awake the national mind to saner methods of curing a terrible disease than by criminal legislation.' On 19 and 30 April Casement made further references to Hector Macdonald's suicide.

In March in the same diary, as Casement's ship made various stops on the way to the Congo, there were references to Agostinho, 17½ ('Agostinho kissed many times,' on 13 March), to X ('not shaved, about 21 or 22'), to Pepe ('17, bought cigarettes'). The very first entry of the diary for 1910, 13 January, Thursday, opened: 'Gabriel Ramos – X Deep to hilt' and ended 'in very deep thrusts'. The next entry simply said: 'Veldemiro – $20'. On 2 March he was in São Paulo: 'Breathed & quick enormous push. Loved mightily. To Hilt Deep X.' By 12 March he was in Buenos Aires: 'Splendid erections. Ramon 7$000 10" at least. X In.' By 28 March he was in Belfast: 'Rode gloriously – splendid steed. Huge – told of many – "Grand".' Like many Edwardian men of his class he was, or at least these diaries say that he was, having a whale of a time. The above entries are merely a small sample.

We are asked to believe by those who say that these diaries were not forged that Casement kept two diaries during his long trips to the Congo and the Putumayo: one long and detailed for public consumption, and also for his own later use when he came to write his reports (the White Diaries), the other short and private, less than a hundred and fifty words per day (the Black Diaries).

This seems to me eminently possible. It would also seem probable that there would be odd inconsistencies between the two diaries: different spellings of names – Casement was not good at spelling names; a few items appearing on the wrong day; some items in one diary not being mentioned in the other at all; a different tone. On the Putumayo trip, when Casement's eyes began to trouble him, he wrote in pencil and his hand-writing deteriorated, but this only happened in the White Diary, the Black Diary was written in pen and the writing did not deteriorate. This can be explained, maybe, by the fact that work on the Black Diaries took only a few minutes, whereas work on the White Diaries was a strain. On the other hand, if I were a forger working on the Black Diaries, using the White Diaries for directions, I would have moved into pencil too, and made the hand-writing deteriorate. The fact that the inconsistency remained suggests that no forger was involved.

To decide to leave the discrepancy you would have to be a very clever and confident forger; but it is clear that if the Black Diaries were forged, then the forger was very clever indeed – a genius. Because there is not one howler in the Black Diaries, there is no entry which could have been placed there only because a forger absolutely and clearly misunderstood a passage in the White Diaries. Although there are discrepancies which come close to being howlers, there is no moment in the Black Diaries which settles the argument either way.

Basil Thomson, who was the chief of the Special Branch created at Scotland Yard at the beginning of the First World War for the detection of enemy spies, interrogated Casement for three days after his capture. Thomson left five differing accounts of how the diaries – both Black and White – were found. In some of them, the diaries were discovered only after Casement's capture, but in one account Thomson said that he was in possession of the diaries for some time before that. Casement's cousin has insisted that Thomson had the diaries sixteen months before the trial. But this confusion does not amount to very much, and certainly does not help us to know whether the Black Diaries were forged or not.

How would the idea of Casement as an Edwardian sex tourist have entered the forger's head? There are some interesting passages in the White Diaries which Thomson had in his possession and could not have forged – were he the forger. Casement wrote with ease in the White Putumayo Diary about 'the bronzed beautiful limbs of these men' and 'soft gentle eyes, a beautiful mouth', to take just two examples. A forger looking at these innocent remarks could get the idea that this was how you could best stitch Casement up.

A possible forger, then, had the White Diaries to use, so he or she knew where Casement was every day, what he was doing and thinking. The Black Diaries would therefore have been easy to forge. It would have taken patience – there are weeks on end in the 1903 and the 1910 Black Diary where there is no mention of sex (the 1911 Black Diary is, I understand, a different matter, but this has not been published), and this either convinces us that they are not forged because a forger would have put sex on every page to serve his darker purpose, or that they are, in fact, forged since a good forger would have known the correct balance between sex and context.

Brian Inglis, in his 1973 biography of Casement, did not believe the diaries were forged. 'The case against the forgery theory remains unshaken,' he wrote.

> No person or persons, in their right mind, would have gone to so much trouble and expense to damn a traitor when a single diary would have sufficed. To ask the forger to fake the other two diaries and the cash register (and if one was forged all of them were) would have been simply to ask for detection, because a single mistake in any of them would have destroyed the whole ugly enterprise. Besides, where could the money have been found? Government servants may sometimes be unscrupulous, but they are always tight-fisted.

The diaries, in any case, black and white, forged or otherwise, were in the hands of Casement's prosecution team, led by F.E. Smith (later Lord Birkenhead), in the summer of 1916. Smith would have taken a rather personal interest in Casement, having himself been a fervent supporter of the Unionist cause. During the trial, the prosecution gave the defence a copy of a selection of Black Diary entries, wondering if the defence would like to use them as a basis for a Guilty but Insane plea. However, this may have been a manoeuvre on the part of Smith, who wanted the diaries made public in the trial but could not make them public himself. The defence refused the offer. Casement was found guilty of treason and sentenced to hang.

Sixteen days before his execution, the Cabinet was presented with two memoranda by the legal adviser to the Home Office:

> Casement's diaries and his ledger entries, covering many pages of closely typed matter, show that he has for years been addicted to the grossest sodomitical practices. Of late years he seems to have completed the full cycle of sexual degeneracy and from a pervert has become an invert – a woman or pathic who derives his satisfaction from attracting men and inducing them to use him.

The second memorandum ended: 'So far as I can judge, it would be far wiser from every point of view to allow the law to take its course and, by judicious means, to use these diaries to prevent Casement attaining martyrdom.' The obvious implication of the first memorandum was that instead of Casement fucking the Africans and the Amazon Indians they had begun to fuck him. The British Cabinet at the time would have realised that this was not in keeping with the aims of the Empire. In any case, they agreed that he should be hanged.

Basil Thomson and his associates set about showing

the diaries to influential people. The King saw them; so did several senior clergymen. American opinion was vital, especially after the shocked and indignant reaction to the executions of the leaders of the 1916 Rising. (These had happened in May. Casement was hanged on 3 August.) American journalists, including the representative of Associated Press, were shown the diaries. The American Ambassador saw them. They were shown to the Anti-Slavery Society, who sent the Foreign Office a six-point memorandum on the issue, one of which is worth quoting here: 'It is unthinkable that a man of Casement's intelligence would under normal circumstances record such grave charges in a form in which they might at any time fall into the hands of his enemies.' Despite the government campaign to vilify Casement, there was a public commission demanding a reprieve, spearheaded by Arthur Conan Doyle. The signatories included Arnold Bennett, G.K. Chesterton, J.G. Frazer, John Galsworthy, Jerome K. Jerome, John Masefield and Beatrice and Sidney Webb. George Bernard Shaw also petitioned for a pardon – in fact, it would be hard to imagine such a campaign without him. In 1937 he wrote to the *Irish Press*:

The trial occurred at a time when the writings of Sigmund Freud had made psychopathy grotesquely fashionable. Everybody was expected to have a secret history unfit for publication except in the consulting rooms of the psychoanalysts. If it had been announced that among the papers of Queen Victoria a diary had been found revealing that her severe respectability masked the day-dreams of a Messalina it would have been received with eager credulity and without the least reprobation by the intelligentsia. It was in that atmosphere innocents like Alfred Noyes and [John] Redmond were shocked, the rest of us were easily credulous: but we associated no general depravity with psychopathic eccentricities, and we were determined not to be put off by it in our efforts to secure a pardon.

The diaries were effective: they prevented a serious campaign for a reprieve; they may have affected the Cabinet decision; they seriously damaged Casement's reputation and legacy. Now, eighty years later, they beggar belief: how could a forger have gone to so much trouble and made no mistakes? How, on the other hand, could Casement have been so stupid as to have left them to be found? It is easy to imagine the forger at work: the entries are short, it must have been fun burying the sexual adventures in all that boring detail. It is also easy to imagine Casement writing these little entries down, his secret life, his private moments which needed to be preserved somewhere, and then almost wanting to be caught, something in his psyche waving away natural caution.

The British had used forgery against Parnell, trying to implicate him in terrorist acts. And nationalist Ireland believed that this is what they did with Casement.

Afraid they might be beaten
Before the bench of Time,
They turned the trick by forgery
And blackened his good name.

Yeats wrote this in 1937. And now, it seems, the battle is still going on: two Englishmen beg to differ about the diaries.

Roger Sawyer, in the Preface to his new edition of the 1910 Black and White Diaries, writes, 'After much research I found that they were entirely genuine'; but a co-editor, whom he does not name, 'made a journey in the reverse direction' and withdrew from the project. In his Preface to his edition of *The Amazon Journal of Roger Casement*, Angus Mitchell makes it clear that he was Roger Sawyer's co-editor until he 'began to have grave doubts about the authenticity of the Black Diaries'.

Mitchell's book is a full and annotated version of Casement's White Diaries for 1910, when Casement was in the Putumayo; Sawyer's is an annotated edition of the Black Diary for 1910, followed by an annotated and edited version of the White Diaries for 1910. The 1910 Black Diaries appeared in the Olympia Press edition of 1959 (without Sawyer's footnotes and clearer readings of Casement's handwriting). There is a great deal more material about Casement's work in the Amazon in Mitchell's book than in Sawyer's, courtesy of a trawl through material in the National Library in Dublin. It is hard to understand why Sawyer did not include the 1911 Black Diary, which in Mitchell's words has caused biographers to pass over the 1911 Amazon voyage, 'as little more than a sexual odyssey'.

Both authors have peculiar things to say in their prefaces. Sawyer thinks that it might have been better had the Black Diaries not been published until the next century, and then justifies re-publication as a way of settling the forgery issue once and for all. 'Inevitably,' he writes, 'much of the detail may be disillusioning to admirers of Casement's humanitarian work.' Mitchell believes that there is 'no need to publish' the Black Diaries 'now unless one wished to throw oil on the fire'; that the Black Diaries 'have poisoned the reputation of Casement and muddied the waters of South American history'. (Clearly, his falling-out with Sawyer has caused a serious outbreak of mixed metaphors.) 'Perhaps least of all,' he goes on, 'do they serve the gay community or merit a place in twentieth-century homosexual literature.'

There is nothing quite like two Englishmen taking a high moral tone. Let us pretend that the Black Diaries were not forged. What emerges from Casement's writing about the Congo and the Putumayo is the extent to which he felt for people, men, women and children, how appalled he was by the plight of each individual he came across, how he hated those who made others suffer. He was 'all emotion', in Conrad's phrase. He loved the people of the Congo and the Amazon Indians. During the day he took notes and statements and worked out a strategy to get the British Government on his side so that he could help them, and when night fell (or even sometimes during the day), he wanted to fondle them and make love with them in a way which would give him most pleasure. Since he was gay, he did it with blokes. One presumes that some of them took pleasure in it too – maybe even some of the ones he paid. On the other hand, having it off with a large, bearded man from Northern Ireland might not have been to everyone's taste.

And more. Perhaps it was his very homosexuality, and his deep interest in 'a certain portion of their anatomy', to quote Eamon Duggan, which made him into the humanitarian he was, made him so appalled. Unlike everyone around him, he took nothing for granted. His moral courage, the absence in him of the slyness of, say, Joseph Conrad, came perhaps from his understanding of what it meant to be despised. He is, *pace* Sawyer and Mitchell, a gay hero. The Black Diaries should be published in full so that everyone's prejudices can have a great big outing. I admire Casement more because of his Diaries. I admire the quality of his desire, his passion, his erotic complexity, his openness, his doubleness, his sexual energy.

Angus Mitchell is right, however, when he says that the publication of the Black Diaries has muddied the waters of South American history, and indeed the history of the Congo. What Casement saw was serious and important and should be remembered. The controversy surrounding the Congo and the Putumayo in the years of Casement's investigation had the same source: rubber. 'In the 1890s it became the prime commodity in the re-invention of the wheel,' Mitchell writes. Until about 1910 wild rubber could only be extracted from remote parts of the Congo and the Amazon, where there were no roads or railways; thus it had to be carried on foot. (After 1910, it was planted elsewhere, from seeds taken from the Amazon region.) It was pure gold for the companies which traded in it. Casement proved in both cases that the local people were enslaved, were constantly flogged and tortured, were even murdered, and that in many cases British companies and capital were involved. His accounts are explicit and convincing and shocking, and because Angus Mitchell's book has no reference to Casement's sexual activities we are allowed to focus on a disgraceful episode in colonial history which has considerable relevance to what is happening in the Amazon basin and the Congo now.

Casement was in a strange position in the Amazon in 1910. An article had appeared in the magazine *Truth* which told the story of atrocities being committed by rubber companies in the region. The Peruvian Amazon company, based in London, sent a five-man commission to investigate the 'commercial prospects' of the area. The Foreign Secretary, Sir Edward Grey, sent Casement, who was the Brazilian Consul General, to represent the Foreign Office and investigate the allegations. Thus he was being entertained and looked after by the very people who were perpetrating the atrocities. He had to keep reminding the commission to take their minds off the 'commercial prospects' and pay attention to what was happening all around them.

On 18 October 1910 Casement saw a group of Indians arriving with huge loads of rubber:

> The little boys, some of them five or six ... stark naked, dear little things with soft gentle eyes and long eyelashes, were coming along too, often with thirty lbs or more on their tiny backs. I saw one lad, looked about fifteen, with a boy's frank voice, with a load of fully 75 to 80 lbs.

Casement began to notice that almost every Indian he saw, including children, had scars and marks from flogging: 'One tiny boy child of no more than eight ... had his little backside and thighs covered with scars – broad weals and lashes'.

> A big splendid-looking Boras young man – with a broad good-humoured face like an Irishman – had a fearful cut on his left buttock. It was the last scab of what had been a very bad flogging. The flesh for the size of a saucer was black and scarred, and this crown of raw flesh was the size of a florin. I put lanolin and a pad of cotton wool over it.

On the same day he wrote: 'What is wanted here is a Hanging Commission with a gallows – not a Commission of botanists and commercial experts.' 'There is no getting away from it,' his diary reads,

> we are simply the guests of a pirate stronghold, where Winchesters and stocks and whipping thongs, to say

nothing of the appalling crimes in the background, take the place of trade goods, and a slavery without limit the place of commercial dealings.

His fellow travellers were cautious and irritating. When he wanted to burn some stocks, the others thought that it would be wiser not to do so. When one of them mentioned cannibals, in exasperation Casement remarked that 'some of the nicest people I know on the Congo were cannibals.' His tone in these writings became more and more indignant and pained:

Alas! Poor Peruvian, poor South American Indian! The world thinks the slave trade was killed a century ago! The worst form of slave trade and slavery – worse in many of its aspects, as I shall show – than anything African savagery gave birth to, has been in full swing here for three hundred years until the dwindling remnant of a population once numbering millions, is now perishing at the doors of an English Company, under the lash, the chains, the bullet, the machete to give its shareholders a dividend.

Casement's tireless humanitarian work in the Congo and in the Putumayo, in what he called 'these awful crime-stained forests', made him famous. He became more and more anti-English as time went on and more fanatical. His health was not good. His involvement in the 1916 Rebellion was disastrous and quixotic, but if the other leaders, equally quixotic, could become martyrs, then he could become an even more famous martyr. Slowly, in the months after the Rising, the British realised that executing Irish nationalists was counter-productive. But they still wanted to hang Casement. After they hanged him, they had a doctor examine him, who said that he had 'found unmistakable evidence of the practices to which it was alleged the prisoner in question had been addicted'. In all the images we have of Anglo-Irish relations over the centuries, perhaps this one is the saddest and the most stark: a prison doctor examining Casement's arsehole a short time after he had been hanged, on the orders of the British Government.

It is important for us to know whether the diaries were forged or not, even if it is clear, and agreed by all, to what use they were put in the time between Casement's sentence and his execution. Angus Mitchell devotes many footnotes to the subject, some of them which seem very important to him do not seem convincing to me, but others are interesting. In Iquitos, for example, the Black Diaries have Casement staying at the Hotel Le Cosmopolite, but he did not, in fact, stay there. He stayed with David Cazes, but to know that you would have to have had access to Casement's letters, which the potential forger did not have. In the White Diaries, Casement used the term 'police news' to mean the dossier he carried from England about perpetrators of atrocities;

the phrase 'police news' is never used in the Black Diaries – a potential forger would possibly not have understood its meaning. There are odd, interesting discrepancies in the account of the interview with Normand, the main villain in the Putumayo, between the Black and White Diaries, but nothing which cannot be explained. There is a reference to St Swithin in the White Diary, which a potential forger may have misunderstood since the reference to St Swithin in the Black Diary in the same short period is, in Mitchell's phrase, 'both misleading and wrong'. There is a small discrepancy about a rubber of bridge, but it does not seem important to me. (Incidentally, Angus Mitchell says in a footnote that 'bridge has long appealed to tacticians and plotters, because of its partly revealed partly hidden nature.' Give us all a break, Angus.)

But there is still, as I said earlier, no howler, nothing which makes you certain that these diaries were forged. In fact, there is one important episode where the Black Diary has information which is not available in the White Diary. It is the name and statistics of an Indian who sat in the stocks. It is missing in the White Dairies, although there is a reference to it. Mitchell writes, disingenuously, in a footnote: 'Casement probably wrote the information in one of his notebooks – a source available to the forger but now lost.' A potential forger may also, of course, have made it up, but Mitchell's footnote is too pat, shows him too ready to be convinced by his own argument.

In September 1993 Radio 4 broadcast a documentary

on the diaries in which a handwriting expert, Dr David Baxendale, who had many years' experience working for the Home Office, stated that 'the bulk of the handwriting in there is the work of Roger Casement' and said of interpolations in the diaries that the 'handwriting of all the entries which were of that nature corresponds closely with Mr Casement's handwriting and there is nothing to suggest that anybody else inserted anything.' But questions linger; why, for example, do we have Black Diaries only for the years in which Casement's movements were known and noted down? Why, since he had so many enemies, especially in the Putumayo, was he never caught red-handed, so to speak? He was a tall, bearded white man, who would have been known and noticed everywhere he went.

Angus Mitchell in his footnotes has two references to a work called *The Vindication of Roger Casement* by E.O. Máille, M. Úi Callanan and M. Payne (privately printed, 1994). In this work, he writes,

> painstaking research has been carried out over the last two decades by two Irish researchers ... Using detailed computerised analysis of key words and expressions they have shown that the linguistic fingerprint in Casement's genuine writing is completely at odds with the linguistic fingerprints of the Black Diaries.

I was interested in this, and I made an effort to track down *The Vindication of Roger Casement*.

I have it in front of me as I write: it was indeed privately printed, it consists of eighteen photocopied
A4-size pages bound together. The second sentence of
the Introduction reads: 'It is important to note that
there were only Two Men involved in the actual
writing of these Diaries, Roger Casement and Sir
Basil Thomson.' (Angus Mitchell in his book writes,
'Sir Basil Thomson has both the motive and the
expertise to devise the forgery' and in a footnote
adds: 'In 1925 he was dismissed from the post after a
breach of the public decency laws.') The authors of
the privately printed *Vindication of Roger Casement*
write that Thomson 'was immoral and an habitual
pervert. He was sentenced for gross indecency in
Hyde Park, London.'

Casement, they point out, was a good Christian and
then a good Catholic:

> He walked the world with *The Imitation of Christ* as
> his companion. Being received into the Catholic
> Church on the morning of his execution, he took off
> his shoes in humility before approaching the Altar
> and last Holy Communion, just moments prior to
> facing eternity.

And then they write about the crowds who assem-
bled for the first anniversary of Casement's execution:
'For all these Christian people, freedom by a pervert
would be a perverted freedom, and not acceptable.'

So we live here now in our perverted freedom.
There are perverts everywhere; despite more than

seventy-five years of 'freedom' we have not managed to get rid of them. (With the help of God, we'll get them out by Christmas.) The authors analyse Casement's diaries and come to the conclusion that they were written by two people. Their analysis is detailed and interesting, part of the debate which is likely to continue about the diaries and about Casement's legacy:

> The Word Frequency Comparisons are remarkable. It is almost unbelievable that out of 1135 Word Frequencies in the Dublin [White] 1910 Diary, all the typical 'Casement' words are absent from the London [Black] Diary containing the alleged obscenities. It is obvious the Forger merely copied Casement's hand-writing, but could only express the filthy minds of Casement's enemies.

Roger Casement's Diaries. 1910: The Black and the White edited by Roger Sawyer, Pimlico

The Amazon Journal of Roger Casement edited by Angus Mitchell, Anaconda

THOMAS MANN:

EXIT PURSUED BY BIOGRAPHERS

A LL HIS LIFE HE KEPT HIS DISTANCE. AT READINGS AND concerts he would notice a young man, gaze at him, make his presence felt and understood, and later, in the semi-privacy of his diaries, record the moment. On Sunday morning, 31 October 1920, for example, when he was still working on *The Magic Mountain*, he went with Katia, his wife, to an open rehearsal of the *Missa Solemnis*, a work which would figure in *Doctor Faustus* more than twenty years later. 'My chief impression,' he wrote,

> was of a handsome young man, Slavic in appearance and wearing a sort of Russian costume, with whom I established a kind of contact at a distance, since he noted my interest in him immediately and was obviously pleased by it.

These were the diaries he left behind in Munich in 1933 and worried about. On Friday, 7 April 1933 in Lugano he noted in his diary:

The news that in Germany they are beginning to clamp down on intellectuals; not only the Jews, but all those suspected of being politically untrustworthy and opposed to the regime. One must be prepared for house searches. Fresh anxiety about my old diaries. Imperative to bring them to safety.

And later: 'They'll publish extracts in the *Volkischer Beobachter*, they'll ruin everything and me too.' This did not stop him making further observations in his dairies. On Monday, 23 April 1934 he recorded a meeting with a Swiss youth, Hans Rascher, to whom he gave a complimentary ticket to a reading. 'I seem to have made a conquest there, or so Katia thinks,' he wrote. It is easy to imagine his gaze, you can see it in the photographs, direct, unflinching, all-embracing, but guarded as well, and melancholy in the knowledge, as he wrote in his diary, that the 'goal, it would appear, is realised in gazing and admiring'. Only a few times in his life, as far as we can gather, did he do more than look at another man. He saved his desire, his erotic energy, his secret sexuality for his work: each morning in his study, for almost sixty years, he unmasked himself, removed his guard. His work from *Buddenbrooks*, published in 1900, to *Felix Krull*, published in 1954, is steeped in the homoerotic. The destinies of most of his heroes – Hanno Buddenbrooks, Tonio Kröger, Aschenbach, Hans Castorp, Adrian Leverkuhn, Felix Krull – are shaped by their uneasy and ambiguous homosexuality.

For Mann being German came first, and he learned, as Anthony Heilbut rather quaintly puts it, to

read German history as one long queer epic – he alluded to Frederick the Great's homosexuality and depicted Bismarck as 'hysterical and high-pitched'. When considering literary history, he enjoyed couples, charging the marriage of true minds with a physical Eros. Thus Schiller's courtship of Goethe; or, likewise, his contention that Schopenhauer had found his aesthetic mate in Wagner.

In this way Mann was able to suggest that his own concern with homosexuality was an aspect of his German heritage, was literary rather than personal. He enjoyed his role of bourgeois parent, loved building houses – he built four in all – celebrating birthdays, taking holidays. Long before he met Katia in Munich he had seen the portrait by Fritz August von Kaulbach of her as a Pierrette with her four brothers as Pierrots. 'The young Thomas,' Katia wrote in her book *Unwritten Memories*,

who was 14 years old at the time the picture was done (I was six), was still living in Lübeck and, like so many others, saw the picture in a magazine. He liked it so much that he cut it out and tacked it over his desk . . . I don't know whether his interest in me had anything to do with the picture he had as a boy. I never asked him about it.

It fits somehow that he imagined her before he saw her. And she records, too, that he watched her ('he had already been observing me at a distance ... he was always watching me') with that gaze of his at concerts in Munich when he was a young novelist and she the brilliant daughter of a rich, Jewish and fascinating family – her grandmother was the leading German feminist of the age; Mahler was a visitor to her family house.

Thomas Mann was both Hanno in *Buddenbrooks*, dreamy and talented and useless to the family, and his father the senator, practical, bourgeois, humourless. In his fiction, he revelled in the drama between those opposites. He combined the Brazilian roots of his mother and his father's Hanseatic heritage: the sharp, steely, distant Northernness of the Manns with the flighty, ethereal and romantic Southernness of the da Silva Bruhns. (This powerful mixture gave him and his brother Heinrich their genius, but for his two sisters, Julia and Carla, it offered instability and self-destruction: they both committed suicide, Carla in 1910, Julia in 1927, just as two of Mann's sons, Klaus and Michael, would commit suicide.) 'At an early age,' Katia Mann wrote of her mother-in-law,

the foreign girl married Senator or Consul Heinrich Mann. She had definite artistic talents, played the piano quite nicely and sang. My husband learned the entire literature of the German Lied from his mother. While she played and sang, he was permitted to be present, just like little Hanno.

Katia Mann's *Unwritten Memories*, prepared with the help of Erika, Golo and Michael, three of her children, was published twenty years after Thomas Mann's death, when Katia was in her nineties. It is extraordinarily frank and perceptive in its own naive way; with Mann's diaries, it offers all we need to know about him. Three new books on Mann, however, each as long as *Buddenbrooks*, appeared in English in 1996: *Thomas Mann: A Biography* by Ronald Hayman; *Thomas Mann: A Life* by Donald Prater; and *Thomas Mann: Eros and Literature* by Anthony Heilbut. Ronald Hayman and Donald Prater are Rosencrantz and Guildenstern to Anthony Heilbut's Hamlet. They are dull and worthy and useful perhaps, and they repeat the same facts and the same narrative. Their desire for Mann to be a better person is almost comic. Heilbut has clearly been to Wittenberg, he can be brilliantly perceptive about Mann's books, he can put on an antic disposition, he can lose himself in long soliloquies about Mann's sexuality and his work:

> Just because heterosexual marriage cannot fulfil him, he inhabits a state of productive melancholy. Forecasting his next fifty years, he finds the Eros life denies him only in his work.

Both Hayman and Prater dislike Mann; they would prefer him to be kinder and gentler, less cold-blooded, less self-absorbed and less single-minded about his work. Prater describes Mann crossing the Atlantic in

September 1939: he holds 'obstinately to his purpose, scribbling on at his deck-chair every morning at the *Lotte*', and writes in his diary that he was 'more and more aware how incalculable, both in time and outcome, is the process that has begun and whose end I can't be certain of surviving'. Prater then adds in parenthesis: 'The supreme egoism here is as remarkable as the blinkered application to his work.' Mann is sixty-four, his whole world has been destroyed. He has the reaction any normal writer might have during a crisis: he wants to get on with his work; and like everyone else, he is worried about what the war will mean for him. Prater seems to want him to join the Red Cross and spend his mornings helping old ladies across the street rather than working on *Lotte in Weimar*.

When Mann visits Germany after the war Prater decides that it is 'indicative' of his 'true character . . . that, with the exception of a brief report for the *New York Times*, nowhere, neither in his diary nor letters, did he record any *reaction* to the vast destruction of his country which he had seen everywhere he went . . . In this apparent indifference was reflected once again the self-centredness dominant in his character.'

'The diaries,' Ronald Hayman tells us, 'reveal that there were no limits to Mann's self-absorption . . . He was never unconcerned with fame, fortune and perfection, but he was compulsive about confronting the reader with his own experience, though he seldom stepped into fiction without wearing a mask.' 'Confronting the reader with his own experience' is a

new way of describing what Mann did every morning
in his study, but his compulsion is even worse than
Hayman realises. In an interjection in her mother's
memoirs, Erika, the Manns' eldest child, says that
'there is a great deal of Thomas Mann in each of the
figures in *Buddenbrooks*, especially in Thomas but
also in Christian and also in Tony, and in all the figures more or less.' He just could not stop.

'Nothing mattered more to Thomas Mann than to win
the world's respect,' Hayman writes, but in the mornings all Mann's life, alone with whatever version of the
self, or of his family, he was creating, a great deal mattered more, as the readers of his fictions, rather than of
these biographies, will know.

Heilbut, on the other hand, loves Mann's compul-
sions, his masks, his self-absorption. 'Throughout his
life,' he writes, 'there were periods when Mann seemed
on the verge of a great confession. His abiding deco-
rum prevented an overt disclosure, but he left his
clues.' He understands and is intrigued by the discrepancies between the public and private in Mann. He
relishes the clues which Mann leaves, and he unearths
a good number of new clues that escape the notice of
both Hayman and Prater. Because his interest is almost
exclusively in the sexuality and the work, there are crucial areas – Mann's political development, for
example, and the fate of his family – which are better
dealt with, however ploddingly, in the two other
books. Heilbut, on the other hand, writes a passionate
defence of Mann's attitude to Jewishness. Mann understood that the Jewish imagination was an essential

presence in Germany. Thus he viewed the Holocaust not only as a tragedy for Jews, but for Germany as well.

As a novelist Mann was lucky that his father died when he was sixteen and his mother was forty. The terms of the will were punitive. 'The estate,' Hayman writes,

> would be controlled by executors, who were instructed to liquidate the company, to sell the ship and all the stock, as well as the house and the furniture within a year. It was almost as if the senator wanted to liquidate the family as well as the business.

Julia Mann had no control over the capital, and was obliged to report on the children's upbringing four times a year to a judge with the interesting name of August Leverkuhn. In none of his autobiographical writings and nowhere in his fiction did Thomas Mann refer to the will. But because of it, Julia Mann moved to Munich, a city ten times the size of Lübeck, and thus all of his childhood and his family heritage became history to Thomas Mann, something he could not have back, something which was gone without a trace. His mother had no objections to him and Heinrich becoming writers. And here was this world, his family's rise and decline in Lübeck, with a ready-made ending, which could only be re-created in words. It was the fact that he was dealing with something so close to him, and at the same time so unrecoverable, that gave *Buddenbrooks* its extraordinary aura of confidence and completion.

The idea that he was not to become a Lübeck merchant, and the idea that Lübeck, like his father, was gone and would not come back, were rendered more powerful by the knowledge that he was not like his father or his brother: that he was homosexual. This knowledge came early to him; he used it in *Tonio Kröger* whose father, too, was a merchant and his mother 'so absolutely different from other ladies in the town because father had brought her long ago from some place far down the map'. But in Tonio's case, it was a passing phase.

Mann put most of his specific erotic obsessions into his fiction. At fourteen he fell in love with a classmate called Armin Martens, an experience which he remembered sixty years later as 'delicate, blissfully painful . . . Something like this is not forgotten, even if seventy eventful years pass by.' He made Martens into Hans Hansen in *Tonio Kröger*. A few years later a classmate Willri Timpe gave him the model for Pribislav Hippe, on whom the young Hans Castorp in *The Magic Mountain* had a crush. When he was twenty-five he had what he called 'that central experience of my heart' with Paul Ehrenberg, a student painter and violinist at the Munich Art Academy, who more than forty years later became Rudi Schwerdtfeger in *Doctor Faustus*.

Even the boy in *Death in Venice* was based on a real boy. Katia Mann remembered being on holiday in Venice with Thomas and Heinrich in the spring of 1911.

All the details of the story, beginning with the man at the cemetery, are taken from actual experience . . . In the dining-room, on the very first day, we saw the Polish family, which looked exactly the way my husband described them: the girls were dressed rather stiffly and severely, and the very charming, beautiful boy of about thirteen was wearing a sailor suit with an open collar and very pretty lacings. He caught my husband's attention immediately. This boy was tremendously attractive, and my husband was always watching him with his companions on the beach. He didn't pursue him through all of Venice – that he didn't do – but the boy did fascinate him, and he thought of him often . . . I still remember that my uncle, Privy Counsellor Friedberg, a famous professor of canon law in Leipzig, was outraged: 'What a story! And a married man with a family!'

One wonders what Privy Counsellor Friedberg would have made of Mann's letter to Erika and Klaus, his two eldest children, both gay themselves, written in 1927, when they were in their early twenties. He had fallen in love with the seventeen-year-old Klaus Heuser – 'I call him Du and he consented to my embracing him on my breast' – and asks his son Klaus, who had met the boy,

to voluntarily withdraw and not to invade my circle. I am already old and famous, and why should you be the only ones who constantly sin . . . The secret and almost silent adventures in life are the finest.

In 1942 he remembered his relationship with Heuser: 'Well, I have lived and loved. Black eyes filled with tears over me. Lips which I kissed.'

His last love was perhaps the most poignant and obsessive, and it, too, made its way into his fiction. Observed by both Katia and Erika, he fell in love with Franz Westermeier, a Bavarian waiter, when he was seventy-five. Heilbut writes that he told Katia that he could not sleep with longing for the boy, although he gives no source for this. In his diary Mann wrote:

> World fame is worthless enough for me, but how little it weighs against one smile from him, his glance, the gentleness of his voice . . . He has been taken into the gallery which no literary history will report, and which reaches back to Klaus H., Paul, Willri, Armin . . . Fell asleep in thoughts of the darling.

He contrived to talk to the waiter about his prospects. Katia and Erika arranged a further meeting for him before they left Switzerland. In a section of *Felix Krull* which Mann wrote the following year he portrayed himself very precisely as hotel guest Lord Kilmarnock (Lord Strathbogie in other editions) who wished to employ the personal services of the waiter Felix Krull. Krull turned him down. Mann let no experience go to waste: being in love with Klaus Heuser was the inspiration for his essay on Kleist; gazing on Westermeier inspired him to write his essay on Michelangelo.

Once *Buddenbrooks* had appeared and Mann had married, his family took on the bearings of a German royal family, becoming the conscience of Germany. Erika and Klaus sought out other members of European literary royalty, befriending Frank Wedekind's daughter Pamela, Erika later marrying Auden and falling in love with Strindberg's daughter Kerstin and the conductor Bruno Walter, Elisabeth flirting with Hermann Broch, Michael befriending the son of Hermann Hesse. The divisions within Germany during the First World War were reflected in the dis-agreements between Thomas and Heinrich. Thomas, Katia wrote, 'for a time believed in the legends of the ill will of other nations towards Germany, of its encir-clement, and of its downfall and destruction'. She insisted that Mann wrote *Reflections of a Non-Political Man*, the book which took up the years 1915 to 1918, interrupting the composition of *The Magic Mountain*, as a reply to an attack on him by Heinrich who 'was so oriented towards the West'. As he wrote the book, Katia said, 'Thomas Mann gradually freed himself from the ideas which had held sway over him.' The fact that he had been a German nationalist gave him a strange insight into what happened in Germany between the wars, and the fact that he had abandoned his nationalism, over many mornings in his study, and many evenings arguing with Katia, who along with her mother had turned against the war effort, made him stand even further outside the world he inhabited, and, indeed, outside the self he had known.

He was more at ease with Katia's family than with

his own; his two sisters and his mother became more and more eccentric and difficult, he would wait until the Forties to portray Carla and Julia, who was known as Lula, and his mother in *Doctor Faustus* as Ines and Clarissa Rodd and their mother, the Frau Senator. 'In Munich,' Katia said of her mother-in-law, she

> was still quite full of joie de vivre. She entertained a circle of various gentlemen . . . and these gentlemen were always undecided as to whether they should court the daughters or the mother.

Carla wanted to become an actress, but in 1910 she decided to leave the stage and marry. 'But a previous suitor arrived,' Heilbut writes,

> and threatened to reveal her sordid past if she didn't comply with his wishes. Although she surrendered, he proceeded to inform her fiancé. She chose to turn this melodrama into a tragedy by taking cyanide.

Seventeen years later, Lula, who had been unhappily married and was now widowed and poor, hanged herself. Golo reported that his father 'was deeply shaken, not because the death of his sister, long since become an embarrassment, was a loss, but because, as I heard him tell my mother, it was like lightning striking very near him.'

There was always a sense with Mann, in his diaries, his letters and his fiction, that he was an observer at his own life, that he had learned very early to stand back as each thing happened, pretend that it was happening to someone else and then store the material for later use. He used his mother's life and his sisters' suicides and his friendship with Paul Ehrenberg ruthlessly in *Doctor Faustus*. Even his own ostensible coldness he puts to use in his novels: Leverkuhn's inability to love in *Doctor Faustus* is perhaps the most moving image in all of Mann's work. In his old age he adored his grandson Frido, the son of his only heterosexual son, Michael. He based Echo, the beautiful child, Leverkuhn's nephew, on Frido, and Echo's 'horrific death', Heilbut writes, 'far more brutally drawn out than Hanno Buddenbrook's . . . stunned Mann's family, already shocked by the detailed re-enactment of his sister Carla's suicide'.

His wife and their six children became his audience: all of them wrote about him, vividly remembering his reading to them from recently completed work. They appear hardly at all in his fiction, yet in each of their life-stories, there are moments and periods which are straight out of Mann's dark imagination, his broodings on sex and death, the German character and individual weakness. He professed to love only two of his children – Erika and Elisabeth. With the others he showed a mild irritation. 'We had once loved our father almost as tenderly as our mother, but that changed during the war,' Golo wrote in his memoirs (the war was the First World War). 'He could still project an aura of kindness, but for the most part we experienced only silence, sternness, nervousness, or anger.' Yet they remained under his harsh, aloof and intimidating shadow all their lives. Michael, a few years before his father died, used to dream about wrestling with him. Both Golo and Michael used to make notes for possible topics of conversation if they were dining with their father. When Klaus was in his early teens his father found him naked. 'Strong impression of his developing, magnificent body. Strong emotion,' he wrote in his diary. (Klaus, in turn, recorded that he dreamed about his father's secret homosexual life.) Mann was aware that he was an impossible model for Klaus. In the years after Klaus's suicide in 1949 Erika became more dependent on her parents and they on her. (When in 1926 she married the actor Gustav Grundgens, the original for her brother's novel *Mephisto*, her grandmother, Katia's mother, wrote that it was 'one of those queer modern unions where it would take the Holy Ghost itself to grant me the joys of being a great-grandmother'.) Elisabeth, who was mentioned with such tenderness by Mann in his letters and diaries, married an academic her father's age, lived in Chicago and Italy, became an expert on the law of the sea. Monica, in a television interview in 1984, remarked that she could not recall ever having had a talk with her father. She did not read the diaries; 'perhaps just as well, in view of his generally disparaging remarks about her,' Donald Prater writes. In 1940, her ship was torpedoed crossing the Atlantic, and she watched her husband drown before her eyes. When she arrived in New York, her parents sent Erika to deal with her: they did not want to be disturbed. Michael, the youngest, became a violist and later a professor of German literature. He committed suicide in 1976, having edited some of his father's diaries, which Mann instructed should be opened and published twenty years after his death.

Erika and Klaus were more impulsive and emotional than their father, enfants terribles at the age when their father was an éminence grise; they were also more secure in their homosexuality than their father ever was; and their relationship with Germany was much lighter than his had been. It was easier for them to oppose Hitler, and to break with Germany when the time came. Erika worked in an anti-Fascist cabaret; Klaus ran an emigré magazine. They both felt, certainly from 1933 and to some extent before, that clear opposition was the only honourable response to Hitler. They were impatient and angry with their father's hesitation. He was loath to lose his readers and his reputation in Germany: he wanted to remain if he could a central figure in German public life and did not relish the idea of exile. Like many people in their sixties he was not brave.

Viewed in retrospect, his silence went on far too long. His children had warned him not to return to Munich in March 1933; they retrieved what they could from the house. He did not return to Germany, but was careful not to denounce the regime. Thus Mann's works were not included in the ceremonial burning of 'un-German' books on 10 May 1933, while those of his brother Heinrich were. In October Mann dissociated himself from Klaus's emigré magazine *Die*

Sammlung because of its strident editorial line against the Nazis. Not until January 1936 did he publicly attack the Nazis. 'I am finally saving my soul with it,' he wrote, 'and unveiling my deep conviction that nothing good for Germany or the world can come from the present German regime.' The Nazis responded by removing his German citizenship and taking away his honorary degree from Bonn University. From now until his death, he would represent what was for him the real Germany; he would be like Goethe in *The Beloved Returns*: 'They think they are Germany, but it is I who am Germany, and if it were to be exterminated root and branch, it would endure in me.'

From 1939 until 1952 the Manns lived in the United States, where his reputation as a novelist was high, and as a spokesman for the German emigrés he became increasingly important. He was entertained at the White House. He built a beautiful house in California, close to other German emigrés – Schönberg, Bruno Walter, Adorno and his brother Heinrich. He began *Doctor Faustus* in California in 1943. Once more he dealt with a world which he could not have back, just as, in Munich, he had written about Lübeck in the last years of the nineteenth century. Once more he used everything he knew, he emptied himself out: his family, Germany between the wars, the tension between the genius and the humanist in his own temperament, his life-long devotion to German classical music, the war, Goethe, Nietzsche, his love for Paul Ehrenberg, his adored grandson Frido. He used Schönberg's music, much to

Schönberg's chagrin – a chagrin which was stirred up, Katia believed, by Alma Mahler; he used everything that Adorno could tell him about music. (He got a great deal wrong, as Schönberg was not slow to point out.) He put large numbers of friends and acquaintances into the book, including Annette Kolb, who became Jeanette Scheurl with her 'elegant sheep's face' in the novel. She never spoke to Mann again. 'He took only what he needed and didn't want more,' Katia wrote. 'He once said as a joke that he didn't know any more about a subject than appeared in his work so he shouldn't be quizzed or examined beyond that.'

People mattered less and less as he grew older. In the United States he was befriended and greatly assisted by Agnes B. Meyer, mother of Katharine Graham, wife of the owner of the *Washington Post*. Mann flattered Meyer in the many letters he wrote to her and had his revenge in his diaries. 'That stupid and tyrannical old bag irritates me,' he wrote, referring to her as 'the decidedly hysterical woman in Washington'. Hayman describes a typical correspondence between them:

> In her next letter, Agnes Meyer reminded him not to miss a talk she was going to give on the radio. Dutifully, he tuned in and wrote to compliment her. But she soon wrote again to complain that he'd never thanked her for the birthday present she'd sent him – a pair of jade cuff-links. He wrote back saying he couldn't have failed to thank her. Perhaps his letter had got lost in the post. But he punctured her pretence

of incredulity that he could treat her so badly when the gift had been valuable enough for a man to live on for a year. This, he said, he could hardly believe. After all, jade was only a semi-precious stone, and he'd seen long jade necklaces which must have cost a fortune if two stones could be so valuable. But he wrote again on Christmas Eve to say how grateful he was for everything she'd done to help him.

After the war he had no desire to return to Germany. 'In Germany,' he wrote to a friend, 'there are two, three or perhaps four people I would like to see again. The others all make me shudder.' He returned in 1949, as his popularity in America was waning, partly because he refused to have anything to do with anti-Communism and the Cold War. Katia went with him, but Erika refused to go. When he told her that Klaus would not have been so uncompromising, she answered: 'That's why he killed himself, which is what I now won't do. That's some consolation but not much.' He insisted on speaking in East Germany as well as the West.

I know no zones. My visit is for Germany itself, Germany as a whole, and not an occupied territory. Who ought to guarantee and represent the unity of Germany if not an independent writer whose true home, as I have said, is the language, which is free and untouched by occupation?

In the early Fifties Mann settled in Switzerland, where he died in 1955 at the age of eighty.

Heilbut's book establishes Mann's homosexuality as central to his work, and there is nothing in either Prater or Hayman which suggests that this wasn't so. All three agree that Germany and German culture were also vital for him. But Katia's *Unwritten Memories* offers insights into Mann's work which are richer and more complex than anything in these three biographies. Mann's three best novels are *Buddenbrooks, The Magic Mountain* and *Doctor Faustus*. In all three, there is an extraordinary, almost obsessive sense of place, and of the characters' lives and habits. These are not simply the characters and places the author has known and loved: there is an intensity in the way they are described which makes you feel that Mann was conjuring up material from a very deep source. Katia spent a great deal of 1912 and 1913 in various sanatoria. 'Well,' she wrote,

> he visited me in Davos, and his arrival was indeed similar to Hans Castorp's. He, too, got off the train in Davos-Dorf, and I met him down there, just as Castorp's cousin Ziemssen did. We went up to the sanatorium, and there we talked incessantly, like the cousins . . . I pointed out to him the various types whom I had already described, and he then incorporated them in the novel, merely changing their names.

The emotion in *The Magic Mountain* comes, then, from his relationship to Katia; the work put into the detail, into the relationship between the two cousins, all comes from her, rather than from his homosexuality, or his attitude to Germany. (In her memoir, incidentally, Katia confirms that the character of Naphta in *The Magic Mountain* was based on Georg Lukács.)

Similarly, in *Doctor Faustus*, Pfeiffering, the place where Leverkuhn becomes a recluse, which is dealt with so lovingly and in such careful detail, and the family who looked after him, the Schweigestills, are all based on moments in the life of Thomas Mann's mother Julia. 'From Augsburg,' Katia writes,

> my mother-in-law moved to the country, to Polling, where people by the name of Schweighardt lived (my husband more or less glamorised them under the name of Schweigestill in *Doctor Faustus*). There she lived only for her children and her memories.

It is an idea that has occurred to none of his biographers that when he dreamed of Leverkuhn's monastic quarters, and the Platonic Germany all around him, Mann was using, perhaps more powerfully because unconsciously, the place where he visited his mother in the summer of 1903. He transforms himself into the visitor Zeitbloom, who would narrate the story of Leverkuhn, and his description of the whole aura of the place uses, or becomes, his emotion around the life and death of his mother. 'Of course I may be mistaken,' Zeitbloom, who believes that this landscape had reminded Leverkuhn of his childhood, says in *Doctor Faustus*.

Pond and hill, the gigantic old tree in the courtyard –
an elm, as a matter of fact – with its round green
bench, and still other details might have attracted him
at his first glance; it may be no dream was needed to
open his eyes. That he said nothing is of course no
proof at all.

As well as these three books a new biography has
appeared in Germany and some new diaries; perhaps
enough has been written about Mann's life to do the
rest of us for a lifetime. Katia was happy that her letters to him from the sanatoria did not survive. 'There
were many particulars in the letters, which have all
been lost. It would be grist for the Germanists' mills to
compare those letters with *The Magic Mountain*, but
they can't do that now, and it doesn't make any difference either. The Germanists do far too much
comparing as it is.'

Thomas Mann: Eros and Literature by Anthony Heilbut,
Macmillan

Thomas Mann: A Biography by Ronald Hayman, Bloomsbury

Thomas Mann: A Life by Donald Prater, Oxford

FRANCIS BACON:

THE ART OF LOOKING

JOAN MIRÓ'S STUDIO LIES AS HE LEFT IT WHEN HE DIED in 1983. It was built for him in the mid-1950s, designed by his friend Josep Lluís Sert, who also designed the Miró Foundation building in Barcelona. It was the space Miró had dreamed of. On the outskirts of Palma de Mallorca, it is a rectangular box of light carefully guarded and filtered from the harshness and sharp purity of the Mediterranean outside. While the Rationalist outside of the building seems dated, the inside, the place where Miró worked, is still beautiful and has an aura of sacred space.

For the first few years Miró found it hard to work in this pristine studio. Even though he was tidy and careful with his brushes, he loved stray objects and began to fill the new space with personal icons. His studio lies there for visitors as an example of the mixture in him of the fastidious, hard-working Catalan and the painter who tried to view the world like a child. He was, like Francis Bacon, addicted to his work and constantly uncertain about what the next brushstroke or the next mark would do to his composition. Unlike

Bacon, however, he was a great bourgeois: his life was orderly and quiet. He faced chaos in his huge studio, but not in his personal life.

However, Miró and Bacon had much in common. They both came from backgrounds which had no interest at all in painting. They both sought and found liberation and inspiration in the Paris of the 1920s. They both learned a great deal from Picasso. They both made versions of portraits from art history, Bacon rather more successfully than Miró. They both invented a personal iconography that became instantly recognisable; and then they both spent years struggling to refine and extend what they had invented, managing and moving on the edges of self-parody. Although neither fought in the Second World War, the imagery in the work of both seems deeply affected by it. For the last thirty years of their lives, they each used only one studio. Both, as painters, were solitary figures who went their own way. Nonetheless, an early flirtation with Surrealism helped them both enormously even if only to alert them to the sheer pleasure of painting to shock and annoy and disturb.

But they had in common something else that is more interesting. Neither was an accomplished draughts-man, and this lack of accomplishment became for them both a sort of gift. By necessity, they became interested in the texture and tone of paint and the use of instinct rather than line or definition. They both denied that they made drawings in preparation for paintings, although they both in fact did so, Miró more than Bacon. (Both made drawings on the pages of printed books; both also used words and phrases to plan a painting.) Miró's denial that he made preparatory drawings was for the ears of the Surrealists, who viewed such a thought-out preparation for a painting as a sort of treachery, a betrayal of the power of the unconscious. Bacon denied making drawings probably because he thought it wasn't important. After his death, however, when his studio was being removed fragment by fragment from London to Dublin, definite evidence emerged of Bacon's drawing.

In his *Looking Back at Francis Bacon*, David Sylvester writes:

> Miró finally owned up; he wanted to show the drawings, Bacon never did. In 1984, in the course of our eighteenth and last recorded interview, I said: 'I suppose it's because you improvise so much that you're exceptional in doing figurative paintings as big as yours without any preliminary drawing or oil sketch.' He responded: 'Well, I sketch out very roughly on the canvas with a brush, just a vague outline of something, and then I go to work, generally using very large brushes, and I start painting immediately and then gradually it builds up.' This was the truth but not the whole truth. He could have told the whole truth by adding: 'But that doesn't mean I don't sometimes do a drawing beforehand.'

It is possible that Bacon did not say this because it would have distracted attention from what genuinely fascinated him, what he really wanted to talk about:

the act of painting itself, its power and mystery; painting as an act of will in conflict with painting as an act of chance. Sometimes in his interviews with David Sylvester, he spoke about chance and will, accident and imagination in specific works. *Painting 1946*, which is in the Museum of Modern Art in New York, is one of his most distilled and disturbing paintings. It shows a large-necked figure with bared teeth whose upper face is hidden by a shadow of a black umbrella. In the background and foreground are sides of raw meat; the one behind the figure is huge and threatening and hanging like a crucifix. To add to the fun, the floor is a patterned Turkish carpet and the background has domestic blinds with cords hanging down. Our friend the figure is wearing a yellow flower in his lapel.

The painting must have taken an enormous amount of energy, both physical and psychic. Bacon put into it what very few artists dare put into a single work: he put in everything he knew. He left nothing, as it were, for the next painting. He exhausted his bank of images.

'Well,' he told David Sylvester,

one of the pictures I did in 1946, the one like a butcher's shop, came to me as an accident. I was attempting to make a bird alighting on a field. And it may have been bound up with the three forms that had gone before [his *Three Studies for Figures at the Base of a Crucifixion 1944*], but suddenly the lines that I'd drawn suggested something totally different, and out of this suggestion arose this picture. I had no intention to do this picture; I never thought of it in that way. It was like one continuous accident mounting on top of another.

This business of how the imagination works in action intrigued him. He loved gambling all his life, especially the roulette table. He remained puzzled by the power of that moment in a run of luck when he felt that something else was guiding him. And not believing in God made it even more interesting, the idea that you could be a vehicle for a non-transcendent force that had all the power of transcendence. And you could walk away with the money, or lose really badly and walk away ruined. Bacon's work in the studio was close to gambling, but it couldn't just be about chance. It had to be precise:

> I would loathe my paintings to look like chancy abstract expressionist paintings, because I really like highly disciplined painting although I don't use highly disciplined methods of constructing it.

He strove for what he called 'a highly ambiguous precision'.

What interested him was not the mind or the emotions, but what he called the nervous system. What interested him was to move so far from illustration – the use of the pictorial space merely to impart information or visual likeness – towards areas of human feeling that he could not name. 'Because one wants to do this thing,' he told Sylvester, of just walking along the edge of the precipice, and in Velazquez it's a very, very extraordinary thing that he has been able to keep in so near to what we call illustration and at the same time so deeply unlock the greatest and deepest things that man can feel.

Sylvester pressed him to say what was the difference between 'an illustrational and a non-illustrational form':

Well, I think that the difference is that an illustrational form tells you through the intelligence immediately what the form is about, whereas a non-illustrational form works first upon sensation and then slowly leaks back into the fact. Now why this should be, we don't know. This may have to do with how facts themselves are ambiguous, how appearances are ambiguous, and therefore this way of recording form is nearer to the fact by its ambiguity of recording.

His painting required enormous risk-taking and enormous concentration to achieve this balance between fact and feeling. He had to clear his mind so that his instinct, or elements of his nervous system, could take over. At the same time, he had to sharpen his mind, use his intelligence and will so that he never lost sight of fact, never ceased to control his paintings. He wanted each brushstroke to combine the lightness of a decision at the roulette table with the weight of guilt and fear and hope that came with watching for the result.

'Accident always has to enter into this activity,' he said. But he was unsure if 'accident' was the right term. He asked Sylvester if he could define it. Sylvester likened it to a ball game 'when you play a shot and feel that you didn't play the shot but it played you . . . and obviously there was no way of preparing for it, there wasn't time, and the very fact that there wasn't time made the shot play itself'. Bacon's reply to this was: 'Exactly.' Later, Bacon denied that this was merely what is called 'inspiration'.

> I don't really know what people mean by inspiration. Certainly, there are things called good runs, when you start and the thing seems to work for you and as you go along you seem to be able to be carried along by it.

The difference between painting and a ball game or a roulette wheel was of course judgement, the ability to stand back and watch and know instantly what had to be done. In every single photograph of Bacon, even ones taken in booths, there was that astonishing energy in the eyes. ('One learns by looking,' he said. 'That's what you must do, look.') When you see photographs of him, it is easy to imagine the excitement and exhilaration of him working in the studio, knowing that every tiny shape or texture or contour he was playing with on the canvas carried emotional weight ('every shape has an implication'). He had to stand back and weigh up and judge, decide before going back, rushing headlong once more into risk and what he called 'a process of continuous rejection'. He faced dangers that neither a writer nor a composer has to face: a wrong flick of the wrist, too much of something, a change that was all wrong, and the whole thing was gone and could not be rescued, as you can rescue a poem or a novel or a string quartet. Painting then was like boxing or batting. He destroyed a great number of paintings, including, he admitted, some very good ones; his run of luck had somehow not continued, something had failed him. 'I often wish,' he told Sylvester,

> that I had a camera and just took the thing as it went along, because, certainly, very often in working one loses the best moments of a painting in trying to take it further. And if one had a record of what it was, one might be able to find it again. So it would be nice to have a running camera going all the time that one was working.

He used paint with immense conviction, but his aim was not colour or tone and he despised the work of the Abstract Expressionists, as he would have despised the work of Miró, as mere design or decoration. Yet he denied vehemently that he painted a world-view. His interest was in creating pictures rather than exercises in meaning.

> I'm just trying to make images as accurately off my nervous system as I can. I don't even know what half of them mean. I'm not saying anything . . . because

I'm probably much more concerned with the aesthetic qualities of a work than perhaps Munch was. But I've no idea what any artist is trying to say, except the most banal artist.

Often he protested too much or paid too much attention to the way French formalist critics wrote about his work. He insisted that his paintings were not violent. He told Michel Archimbaud: 'I'm always surprised when people speak of violence in my work. I don't find it at all violent myself. I don't know why people think it is.' He was particularly concerned that no narrative should be adduced from his use of the triptych. When Sylvester asked him if there was an explanation of the relationship between the figures in the Crucifixion triptych, he simply said: 'No.' He liked doing triptychs of heads because he could use the form of police photographs, he said. And he had concentrated on the single figure because

I think that the moment a number of figures become involved, you immediately come on the story-telling aspect of the relationships between figures. And that immediately sets up a kind of narrative. I always hope to be able to make a great number of figures without a narrative.

Most of what he said about his work was enlightening and helpful; sometimes, however, it was the opposite. He refused to recognise that certain images he created had a powerful significance, perhaps for good reasons wanting to maintain a sort of purity of purpose, at least in theory. When he put a swastika on a figure's armband, for example, he insisted it was for entirely formal, pictorial purposes, and had nothing to do with Nazi Germany. He also insisted that the cages he made for some of his figures helped him solve a problem of form in the painting and had no meaning beyond that. He said that he was fascinated by the Crucifixion, not because of its religious, or indeed anti-religious, possibilities as much as for 'the very fact that the central figure of Christ is raised into a very pronounced and isolated position, which gives it, from a formal point of view, greater possibilities than having all the different figures placed on the same level'.

Unlike his friend Lucian Freud, he did not use models or even do many live sittings with subjects. He used photographs and painted from memory. He worked alone and he mainly painted people he loved. And that, coupled with the intensity of his method, gives his art a quasi-religious aura. (There is no such feeling in Freud.) His lone figures feel like icons. Working like this, trying to find ways to capture the contours of his own fraught emotional life, trying to make what was entirely personal seem magisterial and iconic, applying instinct and nerves, remaining utterly fearless, and doing this every day from dawn until lunchtime from his mid-thirties until his death, all this meant that his life outside the studio – his shadow-life as it were – was going to be untidy and interesting.

★

In the 1990s three biographies of Francis Bacon appeared. That one of them – *Francis Bacon: His Life and Violent Times* (1993) by Andrew Sinclair – was bad can be viewed as a misfortune; that another, published in the same year – *The Gilded Gutter Life of Francis Bacon* by Daniel Farson – was even worse can be seen as sheer carelessness (Bacon hung around with Farson). But the fact that the third – *Francis Bacon: Anatomy of an Enigma* (1996) by Michael Peppiatt – managed to be dull about the work and full of bubble about the personal life raises questions about Bacon's life and legacy. The similarity between the three books is neither a coincidence nor a conspiracy. Rather it is dictated by a narrative that is predetermined: any biography of a homosexual man who made no attempt to hide his sexuality must dwell at length on the untidiness of his personal life and the drama of his relationships.

Something about the way the same facts and anecdotes are rehashed in the three books makes them sound like elaborate alibis. In all three there is an interest in connecting a lurid personal life to lurid paintings. Bacon is presented as freakish and his work as bearing the brunt of his violent and unhappy childhood, his homosexuality, his interest in masochism and his low-life friends. His life, as they present it, is a biographer's dream of a homosexual, from his father's rejection of him, to his sex with stable-hands, to his lust for his father, to his wild times in Berlin and Paris. His life is also full of wild anecdotes and massive drinking bouts, huge triumphs and, simultaneously, incredible tragedies.

Francis Bacon was, the biographers would have it, a mass of contradictions and ambiguities. He was selfish and egotistic; he was wildly generous and caring. He was marvellous company; he was terribly rude. He was half-educated; he knew great chunks of Eliot and Yeats and Shakespeare by heart. He didn't care how his work was received; he cultivated French critics. He had no training as a painter; he was steeped in art history. There is no doubt that there will be many more biographies of him.

And all of these will find the interviews that Bacon did with David Sylvester and Michel Archimbaud useful and worth quoting from. But the vast chasm that exists between Bacon's tone in these interviews – thoughtful, incisive, melancholy – and his so-called 'gilded gutter life' will be, it now seems, impossible for anyone writing about Bacon's life and his work to deal with. In his lifetime, he put off anyone who wanted to write about his personality rather than his work. It is easy to imagine him after six or seven hours in his studio wandering out into London, falling into company, saying anything that came into his head or talking art and books as chance dictated, drinking, spending money, insulting everybody, announcing that he would like to be buggered by Colonel Gaddafi. It is easy to imagine him believing that all this was a way of coming down from his highly charged work, just drift. But the life he lived in Soho and Tangiers and Paris has bred a fascination that feeds into the way we look at his paintings, just as what we know about Caravaggio or what we know about Christopher

Marlowe feeds into the way we think about their work. In Bacon's case, this is heightened by the circle of friends and lovers whom he painted and named in the titles of his paintings: George Dyer and John Edwards; Lucian Freud, Isabel Rawsthorne, Henrietta Moraes and Muriel Belcher. It is heightened further by his fearless and stark exposure of his own face in the self-portraits, especially the *Three Studies* of 1979, and his gaze from photographs. 'The death of the poet was kept from his poems,' Auden wrote in his elegy on Yeats. In Bacon's case, his life has not been kept from his paintings.

Francis Bacon was born in Dublin in 1909. His father was in the horse-breeding business and moved regularly between Ireland and England. His mother's family was rich: 'she came from Firth's steel – I expect you've seen the name on knives'. When the First World War broke out, the Bacons moved to London, where Francis's father worked in the War Office. After the war, they moved back to Ireland. Bacon spent a good deal of time in his grandmother's house, called Farmleigh, near Abbeyleix; his father later bought the house. During what later became known as the Irish War of Independence, he also spent time with his grandmother, who was married to the chief of police for County Kildare.

'Farmleigh,' he told David Sylvester, 'was a beautiful house where the rooms at the back were all curved: I suppose one never knows about these things, but perhaps this may be one of the reasons why I have often used curved backgrounds in triptychs.' Years later he told Anthony Cronin a story about what he thought was a formative experience in Ireland which, Cronin wrote,

> concerned a maid or a nanny . . . who was left in charge of him for long periods when his parents were absent from the house. She had a soldier-boyfriend who came visiting at these times; and, of course, the couple wanted to be alone. But Francis was a jealous and endlessly demanding little boy who would constantly interrupt their lovemaking on one pretext or another. As a result, she took to locking him in a cupboard at the top of the stairs when her boyfriend arrived. Confined in the darkness of this cupboard, Francis would scream – perhaps for several hours at a time – but, since he was out of earshot of the happy courting couple, completely in vain.

'He claimed to owe a great deal to that cupboard,' Cronin concluded. He also claimed to owe a great deal to the atmosphere of threat and violence in Ireland in the period between 1918 and 1923, remembering having to abandon a car with his grandfather the chief of police, according to Michael Peppiatt,

> as the darkness came alive with flashing lights and wild hallooings which relayed the accident from one rebel group to another. Fortunately, the two were able to find their way to a big house near by whose

owners, guns in hand, cross-examined them before giving them refuge.

Andrew Sinclair has the same scene as 'banshee cries sounded from one rebel band to another at the sight of their prey'. All his life Bacon talked to interviewers about this period; as late as 1991 he told an interviewer for *The Times*:

> You mustn't forget that I was born in Ireland where my father trained horses very unsuccessfully. I grew up there at a time when the Sinn Féin was going around. All the houses in our neighbourhood were being attacked. I'll always remember my father saying, 'If they come tonight, say nothing.' He expected to be attacked and on all the trees you'd see the green, white and gold of the Sinn Féin flags.

The Bacons belonged to a tribe of people who, until independence, wandered freely and happily between Ireland and England. England, of course, was home, but Ireland was merely a short sea-journey from home. If you were minor gentry in England, it meant that in Ireland you were grand. An English accent, an English attitude and some money, not necessarily much, would be enough. In Ireland, you could re-invent yourself (as Irish people in London had been doing for generations), especially if you had failed in various ways in England. Anthony Trollope, who lived in Ireland between the ages of twenty-five and forty-two, is perhaps the best example of this. When he arrived in Ireland, in 1841, to work in the postal service, he was the failure of the family and had never written a word. Ireland made him; crossing the sea made him grander and more self-confident.

From the rise of Gladstone and the passing of the land acts and later, from the fall of Parnell until the rise of de Valera, a peculiar atmosphere reigned in Ireland. It was clear that the British were going to leave, but unclear who was going to have power. Disparate forces sought to fill the vacuum, among them the Irish Parliamentary Party, Sinn Féin, the Unionists, Yeats and Lady Gregory, the GAA, the Gaelic League, the Catholic Church, the trade union movement, William Martin Murphy, the rabble, to name but some.

This sense of a looming and unprecedented change, and an almost invisible struggle for hegemony, gave a strange aura to the writing of the period, from the poems of Yeats to the plays of Wilde and Shaw, Synge and O'Casey, as each of them strove in his own way to impose a tone, an attitude or even a set of opposites on the argument. No one in those years was uninvolved. But it was clear to anyone watching the struggle that no matter who would win, two sets of people were going to lose. The old Dublin Protestant business class and the horsey southern Protestant crowd would have no future in the Ireland of the coming times.

It may be no accident, then, that two figures who emerged in the few years after the Second World War, Samuel Beckett and Francis Bacon, whose work dealt in various ways with the drama of loss and despair, and who seemed to view the human presence in the world as oddly and almost comically meaningless, came respectively from the Dublin merchant class and the horsey southern Protestant crowd. Beckett was born seven years before Bacon, who, incidentally, was not a great admirer of Beckett's. ('He wanted to make a complicated idea simple; the idea may have been a good one but I wonder if, in his case, the cerebral didn't take too much precedence over the rest.') Both Beckett and Bacon in their formative years in Ireland watched the power of their class being slowly eroded, lived in houses where there was a constant knowledge that power was going to be turned upside down, that the figures roaring like banshees in the night were winning elections and would not be put down. There was also the small matter of guilt, a feeling that those around them had misunderstood, mismanaged and misused Ireland and were now discovering the consequences. The fact that neither Beckett nor Bacon alluded to any of this in conversations or interviews makes it no less plausible; what happened in Ireland in their formative years affected them in ways that they barely understood and all the more powerfully for that.

When they came to read Nietzsche and hang around with existentialists, both Bacon and Beckett had been through an experience that none of their French or English contemporaries, with the exception of Albert Camus, knew anything about. This, perhaps, more than the curved rooms of Farmleigh or being locked in a cupboard or the rebels roaring like banshees, was how Ireland made a difference to Bacon. Beckett and he were the first victims of the end of the colonial dream; they would belong nowhere as their displaced heroes would also belong nowhere. (The authors of three Gothic masterpieces – *Dracula*, *Uncle Silas* and *Melmoth the Wanderer* – were also displaced Irish Protestants.) Both Beckett and Bacon seemed to crave spartan conditions. The distorted characters they created belonged to the time, Paris and London in the few years after the war, Sartre's *Huis clos*, the work of Giacometti, whom they both knew and admired, the newsreel of the concentration camps. It is remarkable, however, that both of them created work about powerlessness and violence, solitude and loneliness, which seems more iconic and enduring than the work of their contemporaries. Realising that there would be no place for them or those around them in the brave new world of the Irish rebels was possibly the best training either of them could have got.

Bacon was not the sort of gay man who spent his adolescence staring into the mirror asking 'Why am I not normal?' He had, it seems, a good deal of fun around the farmyard. In 1926, when he was sixteen – and this is a story that has all the ring of later embellishment – his father, he claimed, found him trying on his mother's underwear and announced he had had enough: his son would have to leave. Bacon's mother made him an allowance of three pounds a week. He went to London and then, in the company of a sugar-daddy, he went to Berlin where he stayed in a posh hotel. ('The night life of Berlin was very exciting for me, coming straight from Ireland.') From there he went to Paris, where he lived on his wits and good looks. In interview after interview he talked about seeing an exhibition of Picasso's in 1927, 'and, at that moment,' he told David Sylvester, 'I thought, well I will try and paint too.' The Picasso exhibition contained more than a hundred works, including harlequins, nudes, landscapes, studio scenes and paintings for the theatre. There were no Cubist works included, and while Bacon later believed that he saw Picasso's biomorphic figures in this show, (which were the Picassos he liked most), in fact he did not see these until later. During this time, Bacon also saw Poussin's *Massacre of the Innocents* at the Chateau de Chantilly, and he admired and remembered the open-mouthed cry in the painting.

The next thirteen or fourteen years in Bacon's life are a great puzzle. Just as Beckett once contemplated working in advertising, Bacon on his return to London in the late 1920s set himself up as a furniture-designer. The magazine *Studio* singled out his work in an article called 'The 1930 Look'. He was, for a while, all the rage, his furniture was cool and collectible. It lacked angst, to say the least. The Conservative politician R.A. Butler and his wife bought some, as did Patrick White, as did Douglas Cooper, who later grew to loathe Bacon and kept the furniture as a way of poking fun at Bacon the painter. In these years Bacon met two older figures who had enormous influence on him: the Australian painter and connoisseur Roy de Meistre, and a rich and married English homosexual, Eric Hall. De Meistre, among other things, gave him a technical knowledge of painting. Hall, over about fifteen years, paid for everything, including gambling and good food and drink.

In 1933 Bacon painted *Crucifixion 1933*, in which the figure has that eerie, shadowy presence you get in x-ray photographs or photographic negatives. Herbert Read reproduced it in a book and it sold to an important collector. It owed a great deal to Picasso. In that same year Bacon exhibited in a Cork Street gallery in London with Ben Nicholson, Henry Moore, Miró and Dalí. But he had no great success. Throughout the 1930s and the war years (the night before his medical he slept beside a dog which exacerbated his asthma and he was declared unfit), Bacon drifted, painting very little, gambling and drinking a lot.

Therefore, nothing he had previously done prepared anybody for *Three Studies for Figures at the Base of a Crucifixion*, which was painted in 1944 and shown at the Lefevre Gallery in New Bond Street in April 1945. John Russell, in his book on Bacon, has a brilliant account of the atmosphere of this time, when the English spirit was getting back to normal, when a mixture of nostalgia and mild optimism ruled the waves. 'Everything was going to be all right,' Russell wrote, 'and visitors went into the Lefevre Gallery in a spirit of thanksgiving for perils honourably surmounted.'

'Some of them,' he added, 'came out pretty fast.'

More than fifty years later *Three Studies for Figures at the Base of a Crucifixion* (and even the second version done in 1988) is genuinely startling. Although Bacon admired Picasso's biomorphic figures, they are man's best friend compared to Bacon's versions in the triptych. The bodies here are rough beasts, but the ears of the left-hand figure and the mouth of the centrepiece are totally human. There is a sense of an overwhelming pain here, but experienced by a creature who has known language, howling out a word rather than a cry, or a cry that has the memory of a word. And the piece of furniture, like a stand for holding a vase, in the centre panel, offers a domestic setting for the horror. The background (a sort of orange in the 1944 painting; red in the later version) is gorgeously, even sumptuously, perhaps even luridly painted, which makes the paintings look like something wild from a dream, a technicolour hell.

Bacon admired 'The Waste Land' and allowed certain images in the poem to float into paintings. He also admired the Shakespeare of *Macbeth* and *King Lear*. He was fascinated all his life by Aeschylus's *Oresteia*, by the sense of fury in the plays, the overwhelming darkness and the revelling in bloody revenge. He loved quoting the line that is spoken by the leader of the Furies (and he made clear that his three figures in the 1944 painting were based on the Furies): 'the reek of human blood smiles out at me'. For the next ten years he tried to paint that line by concentrating on the mouth (in the same way as he would on the flesh and the face in later years). His sources for this were made very clear by him: they included the screaming nursemaid from Eisenstein's *Battleship Potemkin*, the mother-figure in the Poussin painting at Chantilly, and a 'second-hand book which had beautiful hand-coloured plates of diseases of the mouth, beautiful plates of the mouth open and of the examination of the inside of the mouth, and they fascinated me and I was obsessed with them'.

In her essay on Bacon's work in the catalogue of the 1985 Tate retrospective, Dawn Ades looks at essays by Georges Bataille in *Documents*, a magazine which Bacon possessed copies of, between 1929 and 1930. Bataille's essay on the mouth, for example:

> On great occasions human life is concentrated bestially in the mouth, anger makes one clench one's teeth, terror and atrocious suffering makes the mouth the organ of tearing cries. It's easy to observe on this subject that the stricken individual, in stretching out his neck, frantically lifts up his head, so that his mouth comes to be placed, so far as is possible, in the extension of the vertebral column, that is to say in the position it normally occupies in the animal constitution.

This was accompanied by a photograph of a screaming mouth.

Another issue of *Documents*, Dawn Ades wrote, contained photographs of slaughterhouses to accompany a text on the subject by Bataille:

The slaughter-house arises out of religion in the sense that the temple of distant epochs served a double function, being used at the same time for supplication and for killings. From this resulted a disturbing coincidence between mythological mysteries and the lugubrious grandeur of places where blood flows.

No one is suggesting – Ades least of all – that Bacon stole these ideas from Bataille. There is no proof that he even read them. They may simply show how such ways of thinking were part of the time. Nonetheless, in a few sentences, accompanied by a photograph, Bataille paraphrased what were to become two of Bacon's obsessions. This may help us to understand the roots of these obsessions; but they do not help us to look at the paintings, because Bacon's work for the rest of the 1940s remains startling in a way that no study of its sources can explain.

Bacon's best paintings remain five or six from these years: *Three Studies for Figures at the Base of a Crucifixion 1944*; *Painting 1946*; *Figure Study 1 1945–6*; *Figure Study II 1945–6*; *Study from the Human Body 1949*; *Study after Velazquez's Portrait of Pope Innocent X 1953*. He faced then a problem that all artists face. Since he had invented an iconography that suited his darker purpose, everything for the rest of his life would be a variation on it. Had he died in 1953, say, he would be the romantic hero of twentieth-century British art, self-destructive rather than dangerous, a strange genius who had burned with a gem-like flame for less than a decade and then burned out. He would fulfil the classic narrative of the tragic queer. He could paint, it might have been said, but he could not love, and so he died. As late as 1968, *Time* magazine tried to come to terms with Bacon's commercial and critical success in the United States and could only do so by announcing that this success was

> a telling comment on just how open-minded the general public has become, for Bacon's material is, to put it simply, sick. Bacon, of course, makes no bones about the fact that the obsessive subject of his paintings is homosexual despair. He argues, however, that the despair he has observed among heterosexuals amounts to more or less the same thing.

Unlike *Time* magazine, Bacon was not prepared to put it simply. As he began to work on self-portraits and portraits of friends and of his lover George Dyer, he realised that he was working in a time when portraiture seemed almost impossible. 'The great portraits of the past,' he said, 'always left me with a side-image, as well as a direct image.' The side-images that he sought to create had intimations of what would happen to the flesh after death; if each face he worked on displayed a personality, then this personality was complex, the face concealing more than it disclosed, but maintaining a staunch and at times almost tragic dignity as well as an immense carnality. 'I terribly don't want to make freaks,' he said, though everyone seems to think that's how the picture turns out. If I make people look unattractive, it's not because I want to. I'd like them to look as attractive as they really are . . . What gives the pictures their desperate look, if they have one, is the technical difficulty of making appearances at the present stage of the evolution of painting. If my people look as if they're in a dreadful fix, it's because I can't get them out of a technical dilemma. As I see it, there's nothing, today, between a documentary painting and a very great work in which the documentary work is transcended. I may not manage to produce that 'very great work', but I intend to go on trying to do something different, even if I never succeed and nobody else wants to.

Bacon cited a number of interesting sources and influences for his work on the human body. They included the photographer Eadweard Muybridge's work on the human figure in motion in the late nineteenth century; he took dozens of photographs of naked figures running or playing baseball or wrestling, mixing the scientific and the erotic in ways that fascinated Bacon. His painting *Two Figures 1953* is clearly taken from a Muybridge photograph of two men wrestling, but in the painting they are copulating on a bed with white sheets, involved not in homosexual despair, *pace Time* magazine, but writhing in pleasure, the sort of sexual pleasure that involves legs in strange positions and bared teeth and animal postures. Stuff that normally does not make its way into either pornography or painting. 'It's an endless subject, isn't it?' Bacon said. 'You need never have any other subject, really. It's a very haunting subject.'

He was haunted also by Michelangelo's drawings of naked men, by Velazquez's court portraits, by Rembrandt's self-portraits and by x-ray photographs. Again and again, he spoke about a Degas pastel in the National Gallery in London. 'Well, of course, we are meat, we are potential carcasses,' he told David Sylvester.

> If I go into a butcher's shop I always think it's surprising that I wasn't there instead of the animal. But using the meat in that particular way is possibly like the way one might use the spine, because we are constantly seeing images of the human body through x-ray photographs and that obviously does alter the ways by which one can use the body. You must know the beautiful Degas pastel in the National Gallery of a woman sponging her back. And you will find at the very top of the spine that the spine almost comes out of the skin altogether. And this gives it such a grip and twist that you're more conscious of the vulnerability of the rest of the body than if he had drawn the spine naturally up to the neck. He breaks it so that this thing seems to protrude from the flesh.

In his book of interviews with Bacon, Michel Archimbaud asked him the following question: 'During the few years that I've known you, I've always had the impression that you were a rather solitary individual, not only in your work, in which you stick to your own path, shying away from fashions and movements, but also in your life. Have you always felt this need for solitude, have you sought it?' Bacon's reply was:

> Yes, I have. I feel as if I've spent most of my life alone, but in fact it depends on circumstances. If I'm working, I don't want to see people. That's why the bell at my studio doesn't work. Someone might ring, but I don't hear it. It's definitely much better for me not to be disturbed when I'm working. Perhaps the one exception I would make would be if I were seriously in love, but that's an exceptional situation indeed, especially when one gets old.

Despite his solitude, all his life Bacon had serious love affairs and these remain immensely important for anyone studying his work. Once he began as a painter, his three most important objects of desire were Peter Lacy, the news of whose death was given to Bacon on the morning after his first Tate retrospective in 1962; George Dyer, who died in Paris on the eve of Bacon's Grand Palais exhibition in 1971, the greatest public triumph of his career; and John Edwards, who inherited his estate.

However, 'Everything comes second to my work,' Bacon said. His love affairs, his friendships and his drinking were, for him, most of the time, side-shows. And it would be easy to say that the story of his life, then, is merely the story of his painting. But this is not the case. When he said to Archimbaud that 'a lot of my friends have died. I've not been very lucky in that respect; many people I loved have died,' there was in his tone a sense of desperate melancholy and regret. Both Lacy and Dyer drank with him and caroused with him until this became their lives and eventually led to their deaths.

There is an astonishing painting called *Landscape near Malabata, Tangiers, 1963*, and this records the place where Peter Lacy is buried. It is a landscape alive with brushwork. It is as though it has suffered radiation, or a fierce storm. Once more, as in Bacon's figure paintings, the landscape is cut off from any hinterland or context. It is as if the painting were a glass case and the land inside a specimen. It is clearly a landscape: it has grass, or scrub, and a tree, and yellow sand. Above the horizon there is a black sky, although sharp light illuminates the landscape itself. There is something at work in the very centre of the painting which is full of mysterious energy: black paint rising like a black sandstorm, painted with the same swirls as the tree and a black daub between the grass and the sand. When you know that Lacy's body is buried in this soil, and that his spirit, or his remains, have nourished this place, or disappeared here, it doesn't explain the peculiar aura the painting has, but it intensifies the aura, it helps us to understand why Bacon's nervous system was at its most raw when he set down the frenzied brushstrokes that make this painting; it helps us to understand why our own response to it has been so intense. 'Everything comes second to my work': he may have meant it, but throughout his work, love and grief and indeed desire often seemed to take centre stage. Perhaps the reason why so much of his work remains so powerful is the battle being waged between his own coldness and determination and ambition, on the one hand, and the facts of his life on the other. The battle was won at times by levels of feeling that he did not think he could bear. 'Although one's never exorcised,' he said,

> because people say you forget about death but you don't . . . time doesn't heal. But you concentrate on something which was an obsession, and what you would have put into your obsession with the physical act you put into your work.

After Lacy's death Bacon painted his face on the left and right panels of a triptych with Bacon's own face in the middle. After Dyer's death Bacon painted his face and his body over and over. 'There was an innocence about George,' Daniel Farson wrote, 'even a sweetness which was touching; but his hopelessness made him dangerous.' Andrew Sinclair wrote: 'Dyer had a rough charm and an easy social manner; but he was no intellectual and subject to mockery, even by Bacon.' 'He looked fit and masculine,' Michael Peppiatt wrote, 'with regular features and close-cropped hair, and he dressed immaculately in white shirts, tightly knotted sober ties and the most conservative business suits.' Had he not met Bacon, Peppiatt wrote, 'George Dyer's life might have remained obscure and somewhat depressing.' There is, in all the versions of this story, and especially in the film *Love Is the Devil*, which is based on Farson's book, only a grudging acceptance that Bacon and Dyer might have enjoyed each other, might have been in love, might even have been happy. Since Bacon refuses to play the role of tragic queer, it will have to be handed to Dyer. And he was, of course, the biographers love telling us, an embarrassment. Farson writes that 'Sir Robert Sainsbury described him as "absolutely ghastly", having had the misfortune to sit next to him when Francis brought him to dinner at his home.' All of them rehearse the same anecdotes: a suicide attempt in New York, his not fitting in with Bacon's friends, his mad drinking, his attempt to have Bacon arrested on a drugs charge, and his death in Paris.

It is one of the problems of biography that it seeks out the colourful and the dramatic at the expense of the ordinary and the true. 'The rest of the time, when he was sober, he could be terribly engaging and gentle,' Bacon said about Dyer. 'He used to love being with children and animals. I think he was a nicer person than me. He was more compassionate.' It is clear from the paintings, if not from the biographies, that Bacon loved Dyer's masculinity and muscularity. He loved his face, the flesh on his back, the shape of his legs, the sexual aura around him. He painted him obsessively with pity and tenderness. He captured what John Russell called the 'coiled power' within George Dyer. Russell was a critic rather than a biographer, so, oddly enough, he is the one who may come closest to the truth:

To some of Bacon's admirers, George was a nuisance: an intrusion upon the world of high culture to which 'their' Bacon belonged . . . But it was not in the orbit of these superior people that Bacon would have nurtured the idea for the great paintings that he made in 1966 . . . These were stupendous images, never foreshadowed in Bacon's work and never to be summoned up again. Other key paintings followed in 1967 and 1968, and more than one of them gives us a sense (not hitherto discussed) of domesticity with George Dyer. In *Three Studies of the Male Back* (1970) there was an exuberant power that could only have been born of a sense of being completely and gloriously at home with one other human being . . . As in many another unpredictable but tenacious mating, there were vertiginous ups and downs. George Dyer will live for ever in the iconography of the English face.

In October 1971 Dyer accompanied Bacon to Paris for the opening of his Grand Palais show. He died, possibly by suicide, in the hotel where they were staying on the night before the private view. He was found dead sitting on the lavatory. 'One of the terrible things,' Bacon said, 'about so-called love – certainly for an artist I think – is the destruction.' Over the next eight or nine years, but most intensely over the next two or three, Bacon painted Dyer. He did not need his presence to conjure him up, as he preferred in any case to work from photographs and from memory. His mind went back over the precise circumstances of the death, the hotel staircase, the hotel room, the lavatory bowl.

The saddest and starkest is the painting called *Triptych, May–June 1973*. Dyer is framed in a doorway in each panel. There is a plain, almost anonymous colour for the foreground. The background inside the doorway is black; the walls on either side of the doorway are a reddish colour. In the left and right panels there is a light switch and above the figure in the central panel there is a naked light bulb. The triptych is a portrait of George Dyer dying. In the right panel, he is vomiting into a basin. His eyes are shut, and he is in some distress, but all his strength is there, the muscles of his back and upper arms are carefully painted. There is a white arrow in the foreground pointing towards him. Bacon used arrows for pictorial purposes, to give a sort of energy to parts of the painting. (At times he overused it.) Here it does that too, appearing like an icon, clearly defined and edged. But it does something extra in this painting: it points to the man about to die, as though to say 'Here!' or 'Him!' The same arrow appears in the right panel, pointing at the dead figure sitting on the lavatory bowl, as though telling the Furies where to find him. Or maybe telling us, standing in the gallery, to pay special attention, to look closely. You place an arrow as you would underline a word. And Dyer's body here once more is painted lovingly, his arched back, his thigh and hips, his ass. But his head is bowed, he is broken.

The central panel has Dyer's head and upper body

and the beginning of an arm. He may be seated on a lavatory bowl, although none is clearly apparent. There is a black amorphous shape in front of him, a suggestion of wings, or the shadow of wings, vaguely bat-shaped, ominous. More defined and black than the shape over the landscape where Peter Lacy was buried, but with a similar effect. And no arrow because no need for an arrow. Bacon's lover is dead in this central panel. There is no need to point anyone towards him.

The background of Bacon's painting was, as John Russell has pointed out, half-studio, half condemned cell. An austere, cage-like place. Against this he painted his figures voluptuously; at times he worked like a sculptor creating a monument. (He often thought of making sculpture.) There is great tension in his work between the way the background space is painted and the way he worked on his figures. 'Painting has nothing to do with colouring surfaces,' he said. And he seems to have painted his background with considerable ease. 'When I feel that I have to some extent formed the image, I put the background in to see how it's going to work and then I go on with the image itself,' he told David Sylvester. And when Sylvester asked him if he ever had to change the original colour of the ground, he said: 'I generally stay with the ground because it is extremely difficult to change it when you are using unprimed canvas.' Earlier, when Sylvester had asked him about this 'hard, flat, bright ground' juxtaposed with the complexity of the central image, he said:

Well, I've increasingly wanted to make the images simple and more complicated. And for this to work, it can work more starkly if the background is very united and clear. I think that probably is why I have used a very clear background against which the image can articulate itself.

It is easy to imagine him deciding on the colour of the background, mixing the paint and applying it quickly, skilfully, with a great decisive energy. He talked about it as though it were secondary; the real work came with the figure where he curled and swirled the paint, applying it thickly, working hard to get tone and precision. What he doesn't want to say is how glorious his background colours often are, how beautiful and bright or how pale and reticent. In his *Figure in a Landscape 1945*, for example, the half-hidden figure is darkly ominous and the scene is made even stranger by what Sylvester calls 'the joyous lyrical harmony of blue sky and ecru land . . . an exhilarating sense of the openness of the open air co-exists uncannily with a suffocating menace'. Bacon disliked the word 'unconscious', preferring to speak of the nervous system, but it is possible to look at these flat colours applied ('putting the background in') so quickly and easily as an aspect of Bacon's unconscious, suggesting a pure and sleek imagination that took enormous sensual pleasure in colour and texture, brightness, purity, luminosity. He would have made a great American colour-field painter.

He used rich grand frames and glass, and this way of

presenting the painting helped him to align it to what Louis le Brocquy has called 'old European art'. This implies, le Brocquy writes, 'a particular use of oil paint; not to symbolise, not to describe the object, not to realise an abstract image, but to allow the paint itself to reconstitute the object of one's experience; to metamorphose into the image of an apple, a sky, a human back.'

Bacon was too rational, his gaze was too sharp and his grip in things too focused to allow himself to be called an alchemist. 'The artist's studio isn't the alchemist's study where he searches for the philosopher's stone – something which doesn't exist in our world – it would perhaps be more like the chemist's laboratory, which doesn't stop you imagining that some unexpected phenomena might appear; quite the opposite, in fact.' He continued working until his death in 1992, painting John Edwards as he had once painted George Dyer. Towards the end he even fell in love again, and he died in Madrid while he was seeing his new lover. He continued to add to his store right until his death, visiting the galleries (but in Rome avoiding the original of the Velazquez Pope Innocent, which he never saw), looking at new work, too brave and intelligent to care too much about his own place in art history: 'I won't ever know whether I'm really any good because it takes such a long time for things to fall into place. And there's no point in worrying about what you feel you ought to be doing in terms of the historical evolution of art, either. You can only do what your impulses demand, and that doesn't mean I see myself as the last of a line. The possibilities of oil painting are only just beginning to be exploited: the potential is enormous.'

Francis Bacon: His Life and Violent Times by Andrew Sinclair, Thames & Hudson

The Gilded Gutter Life of Francis Bacon by Daniel Farson, Century

Francis Bacon: Anatomy of an Enigma by Michael Peppiatt, Farrar, Straus & Giroux

Interviews with Francis Bacon by David Sylvester, Thames & Hudson

Francis Bacon in Conversation with Michel Archimbaud, Phaidon

Francis Bacon by John Russell, Thames & Hudson

Francis Bacon: Tate Retrospective Catalogue by Dawn Ades and Andrew Forge

Francis Bacon in Dublin Hugh Lane Gallery

Looking Back at Francis Bacon by David Sylvester, Thames & Hudson

ELIZABETH BISHOP:

MAKING THE CASUAL PERFECT

EVEN IN THE MORNING IN THAT YEAR THE TWO-HOUR hotels were in bloom. The city was full of desire. It was hot. I stayed for a while in a narrow street near the Flamingo Park and went out some days to swim at Copacabana. It was that time between the death of Elizabeth Bishop and the appearance of the first biography and her Selected Letters, when the ordinary reader on the Irish side of the Atlantic knew very little about her. I did not know that for fifteen years she stayed in an apartment overlooking the beach. 'It is such a wonderful apartment,' she wrote to Robert Lowell in 1958,

> that we'll never rent it again, no matter what heights rents soar to, I think. Top floor, 11th, a terrace around two sides, overlooking all that famous bay and beach. Ships go by all the time, like targets in a shooting gallery, people walk their dogs – same dogs same time, same old man in blue trunks every morning with two Pekinese at 7 a.m. – and at night the lovers on the mosaic sidewalks cast enormous long shadows over the soiled sand.

I remember the shock of the first Saturday I was there, how there were dozens of football matches being played with extraordinary speed and ferocity on the beach, most of the players black and beautiful, the supporters letting off bangers every time a goal was scored, and the bangers echoing against the apartment blocks and hotels. They played until it grew dark, and then another drama began. In her book *Brazil*, written with the editors of *Life*, Elizabeth Bishop wrote:

> Frequently at night, on country roads, along beaches or in city doorways, candles can be seen glimmering. A black candle, cigars and a black bottle of cachaca, or a white candle, white flowers, a chicken and a clear bottle of cachaca – these are macumba hexes or offerings, witnesses to the superstitious devotion of millions of Brazilians to this cult.

She must have stood on her balcony as the sky darkened, watching the first candles appearing.

On one of the those Saturdays I saw a woman in her forties kneeling at the edge of the sea and a girl who must have been her daughter. They had left red roses on the sand and lit several candles around the roses. They had left a glass of alcohol on the sand. The fireworks and the shouting from the football matches were over now, a faint memory. The two women were facing out to sea, watching the grey waves come in, wringing their hands in desperate concentration.

This is the space in which the best of Bishop's poems survived. She conjured up what Robert Lowell in 1947, in his review of her *North & South*, called 'something in motion, weary but persisting', and then moved to something exact and specific, something human and fragile, what Lowell identified as 'rest, sleep, fulfilment or death'. She delighted in the exotic, in the passing, noisy, frivolous moment, but in the end her eye was caught by the flame and the woman kneeling by the sea, and in her work she played one off against the other.

In 1985 when I stayed in Rio I did not know much more about her than what she told us in her poems, the short biography in her books and the shadowy figure described in Ian Hamilton's biography of Lowell, which appeared in 1983. In that same year Denis Donoghue, in a new edition of his *Connoisseurs of Chaos*, wrote:

Elizabeth Bishop was born in Worcester, Massachusetts, February 8, 1911. Her father died when she was eight months old. Her mother, mentally ill, spent long periods in hospital; she was taken, when Elizabeth was five, to a mental hospital in Dartmouth, Nova Scotia. Elizabeth never saw her again. The child was brought up partly by her grandparents in Nova Scotia, partly by her mother's older sister in Boston. When she was 16, she went to a boarding-school near Boston, and from there to Vassar College. When she graduated, she moved to New York, and travelled in France and Italy. From 1938 she spent ten years in Key West, Florida. In 1942 she met, in New York, a Brazilian, Lota Costellat de Macedo Soares, and beginning in 1951, they shared a house near Petropolis in Brazil, and an apartment in Rio de Janeiro. Bishop wrote a book about Brazil, and stayed there for 15 years, writing her poems and translating some poetry by modern Brazilian poets. In 1966 she returned to the United States, teaching poetry at various universities and especially at Harvard; in 1974 she took an apartment in Boston. She died in the winter of 1979. So far as appearances go, her life was not dramatic. But one never knows about drama.

There was, however, one piece of evidence which suggested drama. In 1970 Robert Lowell published 'Four Poems for Elizabeth Bishop' in *Notebook*. The first was a reworking of his poem 'Water'; the second poem was more obscure, containing several personal references; the third was called 'Letter with Poems for a Letter with Poems' and was in inverted commas. It began:

> *'You're right to worry about me, only please DON'T,*
> *though I'm pretty worried myself. I've somehow got*
> *into the worst situation I've ever*
> *had to cope with.'*

It included the lines:

> *'That's what I'm waiting for now:*
> *a faintest glimmer I am going to get out*
> *somehow alive from this.'*

The fourth poem ended with lines of homage to Bishop as an artist. In *Notebook* they read:

> *Do*
> *you still hang words in air, ten years imperfect,*
> *joke-letters, glued to cardboard posters, with gaps*
> *and empties for the unimagined phrase,*
> *unerring Muse who scorns a less casual friendship?*

In 'History', published three years later, Lowell improved the lines:

> *Do*
> *you still hang your words in air, ten years*
> *unfinished, glued to your notice board with gaps*
> *or empties for the unimaginable phrase—*
> *unerring Muse who makes the casual perfect?*

These words seemed reasonable: Bishop's poems were full of unimaginable phrases, there was a calm austerity in her tone which could lead her readers to believe that she worked for years on each poem. She sought a quiet perfection, which was remarkable at a time when her contemporaries like Lowell and Berryman were writing unending and imperfect sequences. But the tone of the third poem, in which Lowell had quoted from a letter, was strange, a dramatic, personal and highly-charged tone which had never entered into Bishop's poetry; it suggested that Bishop had an epistolary manner which was closer to Lowell's own work.

In his review of Bishop's *North & South* Lowell identified a banal note in some of her poems, 'as though they had been simplified for a child'. 'Florida', for example, opens: 'The state with the prettiest name'; and 'The Fish' (which used to be her most popular poem) opens: 'I caught a tremendous fish'; and 'Filling Station' opens: 'Oh, but it is dirty!' There were no poems to her dead father, or her insane mother, and her story 'In the Village', which deals with her mother's madness, had to be made into a poem ('The Scream') by Lowell, as though she herself was unable to handle such material in poetry. It was easy to misread her as someone who avoided the personal entirely and stuck to blank description of certain landscapes in North America and Brazil, and whimsy. It seemed that whatever was happening to her in Lowell's third sonnet did not enter the body of her work.

And yet there is a sense of pain and loss buried deep in her poetic diction; there is a peculiar and steadfast concentration in her tone which is at its most powerful in 'At the Fishhouses':

> If you should dip your hand in
> your wrist would ache immediately,
> your bones would begin to ache and your hand would
>   burn
> as if the water were a transmutation of fire
> that feeds on stones and burns with a dark gray flame.

She shared with Hemingway a fierce simplicity, a use of words in which the emotion appears to be hidden, to lurk mysteriously in the space between the words. The search for pure accuracy in her poems forced her to watch the world helplessly, as though there were nothing she could do. The statements she made in her poems seem always distilled, put down on the page – despite the simplicity and the tone of casual directness – only with great difficulty. 'The Prodigal', for example, came in the shape of two sonnets. The first one ended:

> And then he thought he almost might endure
> his exile another year or more.

The second ended:

> But it took him a long time
> finally to make his mind up to go home.

The first ending hinted at infinite regret and resignation in the way 'almost endure' rhymed with 'another year or more'. As a poet she stole a great deal from the dead sound of prose. She made the last line of the poem casual and uncertain, as though nothing was happening, nothing poetic, leaving 'finally' at the beginning of the line like an awkward prose word against the sure-footed iambics of 'to make his mind up to go home'. But the extraordinary amount of emotion in so many of her lines seemed to derive not so much from her skill as a poet (although from that too), but from a repressed desperation and anxiety which filled the air in her poems, a sense of a hurt and wounded personality which sought to remain clear-eyed and calm – 'awful but cheerful' in her own phrase. In 1964 she wrote to Robert Lowell: 'Larkin's poetry is a bit too easily resigned to grimness and horrors of every sort – but you can't have them, either, by shortcuts, by just saying it.'

'Grimness and horrors of every sort' remain unsaid and unspoken in most of her work. Until the publication of Brett Millier's biography, what was in between the lines of her poems was allowed to speak for itself. With the publication of *One Art*, Robert Giroux's selection of her letters, the drama of her life – her sexuality, her isolation, her love affairs and her exile – may take over from the poems. Her life is likely to rival that of Sylvia Plath as a subject for infinite fascination. It is vital to remember the power these poems had before the details of the poet's life became public.

Some letters are missing. Most of Bishop's letters to Lota Costellat de Macedo Soares were destroyed, as were her letters to Marjorie Carr Stevens, with whom she lived in Key West in the Forties. She wrote thousands of letters; Robert Giroux has selected more than five hundred. Obviously, he must have omitted much that is interesting and revealing, but the omission of Bishop's letters to Anne Stevenson, who wrote the first book about her work, seems odd. These letters, packed with insight and wonderful phrases, are quoted in Brett Millier's biography, in David Kalstone's *Becoming a Poet* and in Lorrie Goldensohn's *Elizabeth Bishop: The Biography of a Poetry*. 'What one seems to want in art, in experiencing it, is the same thing that is necessary for its creation, a self-forgetful, perfectly useless concentration,' she wrote; or 'I have a vague theory that one

learns most – I have learned most – from having someone suddenly make fun of something one has taken
seriously up until then. I mean about life, the world,
and so on'; or (in assisting Stevenson to prepare a short
biographical note) '1916. Mother became permanently
insane after several breakdowns. She lived until 1934.
I've never concealed this, although I don't like to make
too much of it. But of course it is an important fact, to
me. I didn't see her again'; or 'One always thinks that
things might be better now, she might have been cured';
or 'My mother went off to teach school at 16 (the way
most of the enterprising young people did) and her first
school was in lower Cape Breton somewhere – and the
pupils spoke nothing much but Gaelic so she had a hard
time of it at that school, or maybe one nearer home –
she was so homesick she was taken the family dog to
cheer her up'; or 'Because of my era, sex, situation, education etc I have written so far [in 1964], what I feel is
a rather "precious" kind of poetry, although I am very
much opposed to the precious. One wishes things were
different, that one could begin all over again.'

From her letters it is easy here to get a complete
picture of Bishop's life, and her peculiar tone, just as
in Sally FitzGerald's editing of Flannery O'Connor's
letters in *The Habit of Being*, a book which Bishop
admired.

Some of the letters throw soft light on the poems. In
'Poem' she described a painting done by her great-
uncle George, and suddenly realised that she knew the

place he painted, she too had been there. 'Heavens, I recognise the place, I know it!' the poem reads. It is risky to use a word like 'heavens', especially if the poet is worried about being precious. The rest of the poem is more hard and exact, but the reader is still entitled to puzzle why 'heavens' was used. The letters make clear that 'heavens' was part of her natural style. It comes up at least ten times in these pages. ('Heavens, it will be nice to carry on an all-English conversation again'; 'Heavens, how I hate politics after the last four years'; 'Heavens, what a vale of tears it is'; 'Oh heavens, now John Ashbery and I have to go and have an "intimate" lunch with Ivar Ivask.')

In 1973 she wrote to James Merrill: 'I could weep myself to think of Mr [Chester] Kallman's weeping over "The Moose".' There is no explanation as to how she learned that Kallman had wept over her poem, which is about seeing a moose during a bus journey. The first reference to 'The Moose' occurs in a letter to Marianne Moore in 1946:

I came back by bus – a dreadful trip, but it seemed most convenient at the time – we hailed it with a flashlight and a lantern as it went by the farm late at night. Early the next morning, just as it was getting light, the driver had to stop suddenly for a big cow moose who was wandering down the road. She walked away very slowly into the woods, looking at us over her shoulder. The driver said that one foggy night he had to stop while a huge bull moose came right up and smelled the engine.

In 1956 she wrote to her Aunt Grace: 'I've written a long poem about Nova Scotia. It's dedicated to you. When it's published, I'll send you a copy.' Sixteen years later, the poem was finished. She wrote to Aunt Grace: 'It is called "The Moose". (You are not the moose.)' She read it at the joint Harvard-Radcliffe Phi Beta Kappa ceremony and was delighted when she heard one student's verdict: 'as poems go – it wasn't bad.' 'I consider that a great compliment,' she wrote to a friend.

> *A moose has come out of*
> *the impenetrable wood*
> *and stands there, looms, rather,*
> *in the middle of the road.*
> *It approaches, it sniffs at*
> *the bus's hot hood.*

Other letters throw light on individual poems, or lines in poems. In 1957, long before 'In the Waiting Room' was published, she wrote to Aunt Grace: 'I spent the morning at the dentist and read the September *National Geographic* – a very silly piece about the Bay of Fundy, but I think I'll buy it just for the photographs. Some of them made me feel homesick.' In the letter she mentioned an aunt on the other side of the family, just as an aunt appears in the poem:

> *My aunt was inside*
> *what seemed like a long time*
> *and while I waited I read*

the National Geographic
(I could read) and carefully
studied the photographs.

Similarly, readers of her poem 'The End of March' will find echoes in several of the letters. 'And then I've always had a daydream,' she wrote to Robert Lowell in 1960, 'of being a lighthouse keeper, absolutely alone, with no one to interrupt my reading or just sitting.' Three years later, in another letter to Lowell she wrote: 'Then I joined [Lota] up there and we spent two whole weeks doing nothing much . . . ' In the poem:

I'd like to retire here and do nothing,
or nothing much, forever, in two bare rooms:
look through binoculars, read boring books . . .

In other letters she wrote about how poems came to her, which makes her correspondence essential for anyone interested in her work. Her letters are important for two main reasons, the first of which is the fact that some of the letters, in themselves, are written with wonderful wit and skill, secondly, they tell a great and tragic lesbian love story.

There are no letters from Bishop about being gay, nor does she mention her personal finances in much detail. She was reticent. But the tone of her letters changes in December 1951 when she sailed to Brazil and stayed with Lota Costellat de Macedo Soares, whom she had met in New York. Even in her description

of the toucan there is something new in her voice: 'He
has brilliant, electric-blue eyes, grey-blue legs and feet.
Most of him is black, except the base of the enormous
bill is green and yellow and he has a bright gold bib
and bunches of red feathers on his stomach and under
his tail.'

Lota owned the apartment in Rio and, as Bishop
wrote to a friend from Petropolis, forty or fifty miles
from Rio, 'lots of land here and is in the middle of
building herself a large and elegant modern house on
the side of a black granite cliff beside a waterfall – the
scenery is unbelievably impractical.' Lota came from
an aristocratic Brazilian family, and was a close friend
of Carlos Lacerda, an up-and-coming politician.
Robert Giroux quotes Elizabeth Hardwick describing
Lota as

> very intense indeed, emotional, also a bit insecure as
> we say, and loyal, devoted and smart and lesbian
> and Brazilian and shy, masterful in some ways, but
> helpless also. She adored Elizabeth in the most
> attractive way, in this case somewhat fearfully, poss-
> essively, and yet modestly and without any tendency
> to oppress.

Bishop was asthmatic and alcoholic; as a poet, she
produced very little, and felt guilty about her work; she
was an orphan, her means were limited. In 1948 she
had said to Robert Lowell: 'When you write my epitaph
you must say I was the loneliest person who ever lived.'

Now in September 1952 she wrote to her doctor in New York: 'I still feel I must have died and gone to heaven.' And in April 1953 she wrote to a friend: 'This place is wonderful . . . I only hope you don't have to get to be forty-two before you feel so at home.'

She began to send letters about her daily life in Brazil to friends: 'I looked out of the window at seven this morning and saw my hostess in a bathrobe directing the blowing up of a huge boulder with dynamite.' She learned to drive and she and Lota owned a good number of fancy sports cars. She described Lota mending a puncture:

> She had on a wrap-around skirt which had fallen open as she bent over and there was a little white behind, dressed in really old-fashioned long white drawers, exposed to the oncoming truck drivers.

Domestic life became a subject for great amusement, as though it was a play she was acting in, a comedy she had invented, something not quite serious, a parody of 'normal' life. They kept servants and lots of domestic pets and a cook who was, according to one letter, 'half-savage and very dirty'. Then

> while we were away, the cook took up painting – proving that art only flourishes in leisure time, I guess . . . Hers are getting better and better, and the rivalry between us is intense – if I paint a picture she paints a bigger and better one; if I cook something she immediately cooks the same thing only using all the eggs. I

don't think she knows about poetry yet, but probably that will come.

They hired a maid called Judith and Bishop wrote to friends in England to say that she kept 'wanting to ask her to bring in the head please'. The cook then became pregnant. 'Hope it holds off till after Christmas at least. I know it's bound to be adorable and I like black ones better than white, even if we are letting the cook do the living for us.' The baby was 'marvellous', Bishop wrote to Marianne Moore.

Her mother dresses her, now that it's cold, in bright rose or yellow flannel garments, with bright green or yellow socks – the father helps crochet them. They are so proud of her that we have to fight every Sunday to keep them from taking her on gruelling long bus trips to show her to all their relatives. It's due to the fact that we supervise the feeding, bathing, etc. There's never been such a fat, good baby in the neighbourhood, and the men working on the house keep coming to look at her and ask about her diet. One of them said he thought she laughed too much.

In a letter to Aunt Grace more than a year later Bishop remarks: 'Of course we're awfully tempted to keep her but I'm afraid it isn't a good idea really.'

In 1956 Bishop won the Pulitzer Prize. By now her three thousand books were in the studio which Lota had built specially for her. She was still in love with 'the lofty vagueness' of Brazil. She regularly wrote to

Marianne Moore about her pets. One 'wild and stormy night,' for example, she lost her toucan.

> There were a few awful moments while Maria the cook, Paulo, her husband, and I, all being soaked to the skin and afflicted with contagious giggles, looked for him – but he was sitting on a little tree above the garbage can, too drenched to fly, poor bird, and quite willing to be picked up and given a piece of meat and dried off with a cup towel. He really must be tough. The cat teases him all the time – takes naps on top of his cage and dangles a paw over him . . .

All through the Fifties the letters were full of joy and wonder. She was a northern woman in the south. Her description of the 1958 Carnival in Rio to Marianne Moore was full of exotic detail. It was clear in all the letters that Lota was now central to her happiness. She wrote letters in praise of babies, kites, cats ('my enormous black and white cat is trying to get into the typewriter right now') thunderstorms, red hair, birds ('one a blood-red, very quick, who perches on the very tops of trees and screams to his two mates – wife and mistress, I presume, again in the Brazilian manner').

But she followed that last description (in a letter to Robert Lowell) with 'But oh dear – my aunt writes me long descriptions of the "fall colours" in Nova Scotia and I wonder if that's where I shouldn't be after all.' In many of her letters there was a sense that her very fragility and instability had made her respond to Brazil with such openness and gusto. In nearly all of them there was an almost desperate urge to remain cheerful. Even when she complains she manages to sound funny, as in her tirade about English washing-habits. ('Oxford graduates smell.') And most of the time she avoided mentioning poetry or writing, as though she wanted to make abundantly clear that she was too interested in the world to write about literature.

In 1961 Lota's friend Carlos Lacerda came to power in Rio and gave Lota a job designing the new Flamingo Park in the city. 'The job is enormous,' Bishop wrote to a friend, 'I went "on location" with her and about a dozen engineers last week – and so far I think she's doing marvellously – just the right tone – but I don't trust these gentlemen, I'm afraid – they are all so jealous of each other and of a woman, naturally.' For the next five years Lota worked on her park, and became involved, through Carlos Lacerda, in Brazilian politics. She was in the governor's palace in Rio when it was surrounded by troops in 1964. Slowly the relationship between Lota and Bishop became difficult and strained. It is clear from Brett Millier's biography that by 1965 Bishop was having an affair with another woman, Lilli Correia de Araujo. Millier writes that Bishop's 'letters to Lilli after she left Ouro Preto (where Lilli lived) in November 1965 were frank and happy expressions of her love and apologies for the sad state her alcoholism had brought her to in Lilli's presence'.

In 1966, Bishop taught in Seattle and began an affair

with a woman referred to as XY. On her return to
Brazil, Bishop continued to correspond with XY as
Lota suffered a complete breakdown. In January 1967
she wrote to her doctor in New York that Lota

> has had violent fights with all our friends except two
> – and it seems they all thought she was 'mad' several
> years before I did. But of course I got it all the time
> and almost all of the nights, poor dear. I do know my
> own faults, you know – but this is really not because
> of me, although now all her obsessions have fixed on
> me – first love; then hate, etc. I finally refused to stay
> alone with her nights any longer – she threatened to
> throw herself off the terrace, and so on.

Eventually, Bishop left for New York, where Lota
followed her on 17 September 1967. During that
night Lota took an overdose of pills and died a week
later. Bishop wrote to friends: 'She was a wonderful,
remarkable woman and I'm sorry you didn't know her
better. I had the twelve or thirteen happiest years of
my life with her, before she got sick – and I suppose
that is a great deal in this unmerciful world.' In Brazil
she was blamed for Lota's death by Lota's family and
close friends. She went to live with XY in San
Francisco and then in Ouro Preto, but three years
after Lota's death she could still write: 'In fact, I see no
end to it all. I try to keep remembering that I had
about fifteen really happy years until Lota got so sick
– and I should be grateful – most people don't have
that much I know. But since she died . . . I just don't

seem to care whether I live or die. I seem to miss her more every day of my life.'

In 1970 XY had a breakdown too, and was in a clinic in Brazil. Later, Bishop and XY parted and XY returned to the United States. 'I think in some strange way,' Bishop wrote to her New York doctor, 'XY wanted to *be* me – and so really was trying to kill me off.' In September 1970 Bishop arrived in Harvard to teach. She disliked teaching, but she found a new friend, Alice Methfessel, an apartment overlooking the harbour in Boston, and renewed her old friendship with Robert Lowell. She had come full circle – north, south, north.

Like all orphans, Bishop was clever at making friends and inventing a family for herself. Both Lowell and Marianne Moore looked after her career, finding her publishers and grants, helping her to become famous. She admired the work of both, and sought in her correspondence with them to suggest that she cared very little about literary fame and success. But the way in which she worked and published her poems suggests otherwise: she waited for years to get things right, but the manner of publication mattered to her very deeply; she worked on a tone which was to be tentative, casual, quiet and modest but which would contain, by implication, everything she knew, and everything that had happened to her. She was pleased to hear that one reader of 'In the Waiting Room' had got goose-flesh on her arms when she read the poem.

In the final poem in *For Lizzie and Harriet*, 'Obit', Lowell wrote:

Before the final coming to rest, comes the rest
of all transcendence in a mode of being, hushing all
becoming.

They were both back in New England now. He had written to say that he had once come close – in 1948 – to proposing marriage to her. In her reply she avoided the issue. It is fascinating to read the letter to him written on 27 February 1970, on which he based his third sonnet to her: 'Well, you are right to worry about me, only please DON'T – I am pretty worried about myself. I have somehow got into the worst situation I have ever had to cope with and I can't see the way out . . . That's what I feel as though I was waiting for now – just the faintest glimmer that I'm going to get out of this somehow, alive.'

Lowell made her letter into a sonnet, just as he transformed the letters he received from Elizabeth Hardwick after the break-up of their marriage into sonnets in his book *The Dolphin*. Bishop was greatly disturbed by his use of this material, and her tone in the letter she wrote him about it proved that beneath all her whimsy there was an uncompromising and steely intelligence.

There is a 'mixture of fact & fiction' and you have *changed* her letters. That is 'infinite mischief', I think. The first one, page ten, is so shocking – well, I don't know what to say. And page 47 . . . and a few after that. One can use one's life as material – one does, anyway – but these letters – aren't you violating a trust? If you were given permission – If you hadn't changed them . . . etc. *But art just isn't worth that much.*

They died within two years of each other. Lowell in 1977, Bishop in 1979. Two years before her death Bishop published *Geography III*, a book of ten poems that might have seemed slight. Before her final coming to rest, after the years of delight in Brazil and then the nightmare years, her tone became more personal, resigned to things, wise almost, so that at least six of those ten poems remain among the best American poems written in the twentieth century. Her letters make it clear what it cost to produce these masterpieces.

After Lowell's death she worked on an elegy for him called 'North Haven'. 'It took me all summer,' she wrote to a friend. She echoed Lowell and used a line from Shakespeare and a phrase from Lewis Carroll, but there are moments in the poem that only Bishop could have arranged:

> *The Goldfinches are back, or others like them,*
> *and the White-throated Sparrow's five-note song,*
> *pleading and pleading, brings tears to the eyes.*
> *Nature repeats herself, or almost does:*
> repeat, repeat, repeat; revise, revise, revise.

She loved, even in her letters, correcting herself, trying to be as accurate as possible. Here, the 'others like them' and the 'almost does' suggest an extraordinary blunt melancholy, the casual nature of death. Lowell had tried to translate Becquer's 'Volveran las oscuras golondrinas' in both *Notebook* and *History*, telling how the 'dark swallows . . . will not come back'. In the version of 'Obit' at the end of *For Lizzie and Harriet* he began: 'Our love will not come back on fortune's wheel.' Bishop wrote in her elegy for him:

And now – you've left
for good. You can't derange, or re-arrange,
your poems again. (But the Sparrows can their song.)

'Will you please destroy this letter right away?' she wrote to one of her correspondents, who, obviously, did not comply. 'Pray for me,' she later wrote – 'and tear this up, too,' clearly to no avail. Bishop enjoyed reading letters, remarking to various friends on the pleasures of Mrs Carlyle's, Keats's and Coleridge's and Henry James's letters, and the depressing nature of Hart Crane's and Edna St Vincent Millay's correspondence. 'A friend of Lota's,' Bishop wrote in 1970, 'burned all my letters to Lota, which Lota had carefully saved so that I could use them – the Amazon trip, London, all sorts of little trips when I was away from her. This is the second time this has happened to me.' In 1972 she sold Marianne Moore's letters to her: 'I've put it off because I hate to sound so mercenary – nevertheless I do have to think of old age and a slightly higher class Old Ladies Home,' she wrote. In 1971 she directed a seminar at Harvard on 'Letters': 'Just *letters* – as an art form or something. I'm hoping to select a nicely incongruous assortment of people – Mrs Carlyle, Chekhov, my Aunt Grace, Keats, a letter found in the street, etc etc.' The letter was, she said, 'the dying form of communication'. Most of her letters read like performances, bursts of energy, full of delight at the quirky and the exotic; full of 'fun' (she tended to put 'fun' in inverted commas – '"fun"', she wrote in her elegy to Lowell, 'it always seemed to leave you at a loss.') But others break down into pure confession, and are heartbreaking in their honesty. 'I am sorry for people who can't write letters,' Bishop wrote. 'But I suspect that you and I love to write them because it's kind of like working without really doing it.'

One Art: The Selected Letters of Elizabeth Bishop edited by Robert Giroux, Chatto

Elizabeth Bishop: Life and the Memory of It by Brett Millier, University of California Press

JAMES BALDWIN:

THE FLESH AND THE DEVIL

O N THE FIRST OF FEBRUARY 2001 IN THE ALICE TULLY
Hall in the Lincoln Centre in New York eight
writers came to pay homage to James Baldwin. The
event was booked out and there were people standing
outside desperately looking for tickets. The audience
was strange; in general in New York an audience is
either young or old (in the Lincoln Centre mainly old),
black or white (in the Lincoln Centre, almost exclusively white), gay or straight (in the Lincoln Centre it
was often hard to tell). The audience for James
Baldwin that evening, however, could not be so easily
categorised: it was, I suppose, half black, half white;
half young, half old; three-quarters straight, a quarter
gay. But many of those who had come carried with
them, in their faces and their body language, a sense
that there were more important things than age or race
or sexuality. Also, there was a large number of young
black men who had come alone, who carried a book
and an aura of seriousness and intensity. There was a
good number of writers. Some of Baldwin's family was
there.

The speeches made it clear that James Baldwin's legacy is both powerful and fluid, allowing it to fit whatever category each reader requires, allowing it to influence each reader in a way which tells us as much about the reader as it does about Baldwin.

And what it tells us about Baldwin has to do with his contradictions, the large set of opposites which made up his personality. He was, for some of his life, a pure artist, using Jamesian techniques and cadences. He was also an agitator and a propagandist, political and engaged. He was steeped in the world of his childhood in Harlem. He also loved the bohemian world of Greenwich Village and Paris. He was a loner. He was also a deeply gregarious and social being. He was the most eloquent man in the America of his time. His legacy is also one of failure. It is hard to decide what part of him came first. Was the colour of his skin more important than his sexuality? Was his religious upbringing more important than his reading of the American masters? Were his sadness and anger more important than his love of laughter, his delight in the world? Did his prose style, as the novelist Russell Banks claimed that evening, take its bearings from Emerson, or was it, according to the writer Hilton Als who also spoke, 'a high-faggot style', or did it originate, as John Edgar Wideman claimed, from a mixture of the King James Bible and African-American speech? Was it full of the clarity, eloquence and intelligence that Chinua Achebe suggested? And was Baldwin's involvement with the Civil Rights movement a cautionary tale for other writers, as Hilton Als insisted, or was it one of the reasons we should most admire him, as Amiri Baraka argued? Is his best book the book that has not yet appeared – a volume of his letters – as Hilton Als proposed, or are his essays his finest work, as many now believe, or are his early novels his enduring legacy, books which 'blew my mind', as Chinua Achebe said that evening?

For all of the speakers, and indeed for the audience, the relationship to Baldwin's work remains intense. The complexity of Baldwin's character, the power of his prose-style and the abiding importance of his subjects make him a writer to confront and argue with as well as a writer to admire. Out of his arguments with himself, he made his essays, and this gives them a riveting honesty and edge. In his novels, he sought to explore the parts of the self which most of us seek to conceal. And he was also concerned with style, with how you write a sentence, how you control the music and rhythms of prose.

James Baldwin was born in Harlem in 1924. He was the eldest of a large family. His father died when he was nineteen. 'On the same day,' Baldwin wrote in *Notes of a Native Son*, 'a few hours later, his last child was born. Over a month before this, while all our energies were concentrated in waiting for these events, there had been, in Detroit, one of the bloodiest race riots of the century. A few hours after my father's funeral, while he lay in state in the undertaker's chapel, a race riot broke out in Harlem . . . As we drove him to the graveyard, the spoils of injustice, anarchy, discontent and hatred were all around us.'

Baldwin began with a very great subject: the drama of his own life matching or echoing against the public drama. He also began with certain influences. When he was thirty-one years old, he listed them in *Notes of a Native Son*: 'the King James Bible, the rhetoric of the store-front church, something ironic and violent and perpetually understated in Negro speech – and something of Dicken's love for bravura.'

However, he added something of his own to his inherited subject and the influences he listed. It was something so all-pervasive in his work, both his essays and his fiction, that he may not have even noticed it, and certainly did not want to write about it. He used and adapted the tone of the great masters of English eloquence: Bacon, Sir Thomas Browne, Hazlitt, Emerson and Henry James. He brought, he wrote, 'a special attitude' to 'Shakespeare, Bach, Rembrandt, to the stones of Paris, to the cathedral of Chartres, and to the Empire State Building . . . These were not really my creations; they did not contain my history; I might search in vain forever for any reflection of myself. I was an interloper; this was not my heritage. At the same time I had no other heritage which I could possibly hope to use – I had certainly been unfitted for the jungle and the tribe. I would have to appropriate those white centuries, I would have to make them mine.'

By appropriating the heritage of English prose, Baldwin learned not only a style but also a cast of mind. The cast of mind used qualification, the aside and the further sub-clauses as a way to suggest that the truth was brittle and easily undermined. His prose played with the explicit and the implicit, the bald statement and the skeptical gloss. His style could be high and grave and reflect the glittering mind; his thought was embodied beautifully in his style, as though fresh language had led him to fresh thought. From Henry James, he also learned a great deal about character and consciousness in fiction, the use of the single point of view, the use of nuance and shade.

He had, early in his career, what Eliot said about James, 'a mind so fine that it could not be penetrated by an idea'; and the rest of the time he did not have this luxury, as public events, and indeed private ones, pressed in on his imagination, forbade him the sort of freedom he naturally sought. He was both freed and cornered by his heritage, freed from being a dandy and freed into finding a subject, and then cornered into being a spokesman or an exile, cornered into anger.

In his speech that evening in the Lincoln Centre, Chinua Achebe spoke of an uncanny connection between his work and that of Baldwin. In *Things Fall Apart*, the portrait of the father's anger and power-lessness is very close to the portrait of the father in Baldwin's essays and his fiction. That this father who died when Baldwin was nineteen was not really his father – he never knew the name of his real father – made his regret at not knowing him and not liking him all the greater.

Hansome, proud, and ingrown, 'like a toenail', some-body said. But he looked to me, as I grew older, like pictures I had seen of African tribal chieftains: he really should have been naked, with war paint on and barbaric mementos, standing among spears. He could be chilling in the pulpit and indescribably cruel in his personal life and he was certainly the most bitter man I have ever met . . . When he died I had been away from home for a little over a year . . . I had discovered the weight of white people in the world. I saw that this had been for my ancestors and now would be for me an awful thing to live with and that the bitterness which had helped to kill my father could also kill me.

Baldwin's bitterness was fired by working in a defence plant in New Jersey during the war, and learning that 'bars, bowling alleys, diners, places to live' were closed to him. There was something about him that made him insist on going into these places, suffer rejection, forcing them to refuse to serve him. He described his last night there when, having been refused in a diner, he went into 'an enormous, glittering and fashionable restaurant in which I knew not even the intercession of the Virgin would cause me to be served'. He sat at a table until a waitress came and said: 'We don't serve Negroes here.' He noted the fear and the apology in her voice. 'I wanted her to come close enough for me to get her neck between my hands.' Instead, he threw a half-full watermug at her and missed and ran. Later, he realised that he had been ready to commit murder. I saw nothing very clearly, but I did see this: that my life, my *real* life, was in danger, and not from anything other people might do but from the hatred I carried in my own heart.

Baldwin published this in 1955 when he was thirty-one. His tone in these early essays was not simply political; he was not demanding legislation or urgent government action. He did not present himself as innocent and the others as guilty. He sought to do something more truthful and difficult. He sought to show that the damage had entered his soul from where it could not be easily dislodged, and he sought also to show that the soul of America itself was a great stained soul. He shook his head at the possibility that anything other than mass conversion could change things. He had not been a child preacher for nothing.

How he moved from raw anger to becoming one of the finest prose-stylists of the age remains fascinating. He moved downtown after his father died and began to hang out in Greenwich Village. 'There were very few black people in the Village in those years,' he wrote in 1985,

and of that handful, I was decidedly, the most improbable . . . I was eager, vulnerable and lonely . . . I am sure that I was afraid that I already seemed and sounded too much like a woman. In my childhood, at least until my adolescence, my playmates had called me a sissy . . . On every street corner, I was called a faggot.

He found odd jobs and then lost them, washing dishes, working as an elevator boy. He drank, he had casual affairs, he suffered a number of nervous crises. The five years between the death of his father and his leaving New York remained for him nightmare years where he came within a breath of self-destruction.

The colour of his skin caused him, in both his essays and his fiction, to create a version of America which was passionate and original; his homosexuality caused a similar attempt to describe and dramatise the sexual politics of his time. 'The American *ideal*, then, of sexuality appears to be rooted in the American idea of masculinity,' he wrote in 1985,

> This ideal had created cowboys and Indians, good guys and bad guys, punks and studs, tough guys and softies, butch and faggot, black and white. It is an ideal so paralytically infantile that it is virtually forbidden – as an unpatriotic act – that the American boy evolve into the complexity of manhood.

In an essay on Richard Wright, published in 1951, Baldwin wrote:

> And there is, I should think no Negro living in America who has not felt briefly and for long periods, with anguish sharp or dull, in varying degrees or to varying effect, simple, naked and unanswerable hatred; who has not wanted to smash any white face he may encounter in a day, to violate, out of motives of the cruelest vengeance, their women, to break the

bodies of all white people and bring them low, as low as that dust into which he himself has been and is being trampled.

In 1962, Baldwin published *Another Country* which dealt with masculinity and race and rage and the fate of a young musician from Harlem who had dared to live in Greenwich Village. Rufus, who is the central character in *Another Country*, has felt hatred and been brushed by its wings, but Baldwin was too subtle and alert to the danger of making him merely an angry black man, or a victim. In an essay in 1960 called 'Notes for a Hypothetical Novel' he had mused on the white people he met in downtown New York in his early twenties:

> In the beginning, I thought that the white world was very different from the world I was moving out of and I turned out to be entirely wrong. It seemed different. It seemed safer, at least the white people seemed safer. It seemed cleaner, it seemed more polite, and, of course, it seemed much richer from the material point of view. But I didn't meet anyone in that world who didn't suffer from the same affliction that all the people I had fled from suffered from and that was that they didn't know who they were. They wanted to be someone that they were not.

Baldwin knew to make his hero bad as well as brilliant, to place a violent and self-destructive charm at the core of him and to make his white friends uneasy and complex figures too, unable to protect themselves. The first eighty pages of the book are astonishing, as we watch Rufus move towards his doom. In 1960 in an essay Baldwin had alluded to the 'body of sexual myths . . . around the figure of the American Negro' who 'is penalised for the guilty imagination of the white people who invest him with their hates and longings, and is the principal target of their sexual longings.' Rufus is aware of this and suspicious of his own attractions. He will grow to hate the white woman who wants him. He will grow to despise and distrust his white friends. He will walk the city, destitute and forlorn. He will do what Baldwin's friend Eugene Worth did in 1946, he will finally jump to his death off the George Washington Bridge. 'There are no antecedents for [Rufus],' Baldwin later said.

> He was in the novel because I don't think anyone had ever watched the disintegration of a black boy from that particular point of view. Rufus was partly responsible for his doom, and in presenting him as partly responsible, I was attempting to break out of the whole sentimental image of the afflicted nigger driven that way (to suicide) by white people.

Rufus is a tragic hero caught between the time when men such as him had no freedom, and the time to come. The city has opened its doors to him, not enough for him to feel free, but just enough for him to feel danger and threat. He is like someone who has been released from solitary confinement into the wider prison.

Two years after the suicide of Eugene Worth, Baldwin left New York and moved to Paris. 'I didn't know what was going to happen to me in Paris,' he told the *Paris Review*, 'but I knew what was going to happen to me in New York. If I had stayed there, I would have gone under, like my friend on the George Washington Bridge.'

'I left America,' he wrote in 1959, 'because I doubted my ability to survive the fury of the colour problem here . . . I wanted to prevent myself from becoming *merely* a Negro; or even merely a Negro writer.' The fate of Eugene Worth continued to haunt him. He wrote in 1961: 'I felt then, and, to tell the truth, I feel now that he would not have died in such a way and certainly not so soon, if he had not been black.' In that year Baldwin also wrote: 'My revenge, I decided very early, would be to achieve a power which outlasts kingdoms . . . To become a Negro man, let alone a Negro artist, one has to make oneself up as one went along.'

He invented for himself two role models. One was the painter Beauford Delaney whom Baldwin first visited in his studio in Greenwich Village when Baldwin was sixteen and was still a child preacher. 'Beauford was the first walking, living proof, for me, that a black man could be an artist.' Four years later, Baldwin met Richard Wright, who was sixteen years older than him and, at that time, the most famous black writer in

America. Wright encouraged Baldwin, read his work and recommended him for a grant. And, just as important, Wright offered him an example by going to live in Paris in 1946. (Beauford Delaney also moved there in 1952.) When Baldwin arrived in Paris in November 1948, he found Richard Wright sitting at a table in Saint-Germain. Wright found him somewhere to stay and introduced him to the world of expatriate bohemia in Paris.

Over the next six years, which were spent mostly in Paris, James Baldwin produced two novels, *Go Tell It On The Mountain* and *Giovanni's Room*, some of his best stories, and his first book of essays, *Notes of a Native Son*, made up of pieces mainly published in *Partisan Review*, *Commentary* and *Harper's*.

It would be easy to argue that *Go Tell It On The Mountain* and *Giovanni's Room* were written by different people, one the young writer whose imagination was fired by his childhood and its discontents, who had observed the older generation in his family, had come to understand them better than he did himself, so that he could draw them with raw sympathy in a language which was richly charged. In his first novel, Baldwin was concerned with their sensuality, their flesh as both a badge of glorious self and a source of shame and sinfulness. He tried to capture them in the most beautiful sentences, and tried to fill their relationships, their privacies, their motives and their thought processes with nuance and qualification, with subtlety and well-wrought cadence. Henry James had come to Harlem. The novel was finished in 1952, accepted by Knopf and published the following year.

The arrival of Baldwin the essayist and novelist was greeted with joy and relief by the New York editors he wrote for. Someone had arrived who could write wonderful prose, who had a sense of politics and the destiny of his people, who was both wise and smart, who was from Harlem but had developed other perspectives, and whose first novel, in its treatment of religion and a Harlem only barely understood south of one hundred and twenty-fifth street, was compared to William James and William Faulkner. In 1950, Baldwin in Paris had read James Joyce's *A Portrait of the Artist as a Young Man*, whose story was not lost on him. The need to do battle with religion and his own oppressed nation, some of whose members were unhappy with his novel and his attitudes; the need to go into exile; the need to create a voice and mode of perception for a sensitive, literary young man; these became Baldwin's needs as much as Joyce's. 'What I mainly learned [in France],' he later said, 'was about my own country, my own past, and about my own language. Joyce accepted silence, exile and cunning as a system which would sustain his life, and I've had to accept it too – incidentally, silence is the hardest part to understand.'

Baldwin's editors and reviewers would have been happy had he gone on now to recreate the conscience of his race in book after book. But two things were to interest him and these would interrupt what looked in 1955, with the publication of *Notes of a Native Son*,

to be a brilliant career. The first was his own homosexuality and the second was the Civil Rights
Movement.

In 1951 Baldwin published an early story 'The
Outing', which remains one of his best stories. The
church community which appears in *Go Tell It On
The Mountain* go on an outing on a boat up the
Hudson River. The story concentrates on a number of
adolescent boys who are part of the church. It ends as
follows:

> All during the trip home David seemed preoccupied.
> When he finally sought out Johnnie he found him sit-
> ting by himself on the top deck, shivering a little in
> the night air. He sat down beside him. After a
> moment Johnnie moved and put his head on David's
> shoulder. David put his arms around him. But now
> where there had been peace there was only panic and
> where there had been safety, danger, like a flower,
> opened.

This was dangerous territory in 1951. By this time
Baldwin had fallen in love with a Swiss man living in
Paris, Lucien Happersberger, and, despite the fact that
Happersberger soon got married, Baldwin would
remain involved with him, in various ways, for the
rest of his life. The relationship between the two men
and between Baldwin and a number of close women
friends, and the general air of sexual ambivalence and

dishonesty in Greenwich Village and Paris gave Baldwin the atmosphere for *Giovanni's Room*. 'Specifically,' David Leeming wrote in his biography,

> it reflects his own wrestling with sexual ambivalence. Like David [in the novel], he had been engaged or nearly engaged. He, too . . . had tried to convince himself of his essential heterosexuality. But unlike David, he had willingly accepted the reality represented by Giovanni's room when it came to him in the person of Lucien, to whom he dedicated the novel. Ironically, it was Lucien who married and who, several times over the years, rejected the room to which Jimmy called him and who, in Jimmy's eyes, became David to his Giovanni.

For his editors in New York, publishing a black writer was fascinating, but publishing a black homosexual writer was impossible. And there were no black characters at all in Baldwin's second novel. There was nothing about 'the Negro problem'. Thirty years later, in a *Paris Review* interview, Baldwin said: 'The sexual-moral light was a hard thing to deal with. I could not handle both propositions in the same book.' Knopf turned the book down. Baldwin's agent advised him to burn it. 'When I turned the book in,' Baldwin later said,

> I was told I shouldn't have written it. I was told to bear in mind that I was a young Negro writer with a certain audience and I wasn't supposed to alienate the

audience. And if I published the book, it would wreck my career. They wouldn't publish the book, they said, as a favour to me.

In London, however, Michael Joseph agreed to publish *Giovanni's Room* and, later, in New York, a small publisher, the Dial Press, offered to bring the book out. It first appeared in 1956.

Both *Go Tell It On The Mountain* and *Giovanni's Room* were declarations of independence for Baldwin. In the first, he dramatised the destiny of a black family in Harlem, but he refused to allow that destiny to be shaped by an obvious plot in which being black could only lead to mayhem and tragedy. It is as much a landmark in American writing as Joyce's *Dubliners* was in Ireland. *Dubliners* refused to allow its characters to have their destiny shaped directly by Irish history or the land wars or the British presence in Irish writing. Both Joyce's characters and Baldwin's characters suffer because of what is within them.

In placing the very nature of his characters, their inner demons, at the centre, Baldwin refused to write a parable of race relations. His theory for this refusal appeared some years before *Go Tell It On The Mountain*, in two essays – 'Everybody's Protest Novel' (1949) and 'Many Thousands Gone' (1951). Both were essentially attacks on Richard Wright's novel *Native Son*.

All of Bigger's [the black hero who commits a murder at the end of the book] life is controlled, defined by his hatred and his fear. And later his fear drives him to murder and his hatred to rape . . . Below the surface of this novel there lies, as it seems to me, a continuation, a complement of that monstrous legend it was written to destroy.

In prose which was rich and allusive, Baldwin characterised *Native Son* as a protest novel whose

climate of anarchy and unmotivated and unapprehended disaster . . . has led us all to believe that in Negro life there exists no tradition, no field of manners, no possibility of ritual and intercourse . . . But the fact is not that the Negro has no tradition but that there has as yet arrived no sensibility sufficiently profound and tough to make this tradition articulate.

In writing *Giovanni's Room*, Baldwin further emphasised that he was profound and tough enough to declare his further independence from what others might have called his heritage, his natural subject matter. For a black man to decide to write a novel with mainly gay white characters, set in France, was a brave political act. To place a murder, however, at the centre of his gay plot was to do to homosexuals what he had attacked Wright for doing to black people – adding impetus to the popular notion that they were alarming. Needless to say, there was no one to point this out at the time.

Baldwin at his best has two voices. One is the third-person narrative of his first novel and the opening chapters of *Another Country*. The prose is dense; there is a fierce concentration on the single consciousness; the tone is relentless. The second voice is his own first-person voice, the voice of his essays. This voice is earnest, it deals in difficult truths and it has an urgent edge to it, but it manages to be personal and private, a tone which whispers and insinuates rather than hectors.

The power of this second voice makes the first-person voices Baldwin created for his fictional characters in *Giovanni's Room*, *Tell Me How Long The Train's Been Gone* (1968), 'If Beale Street Could Talk' (1974), 'Just Above My Head' (1978) and some of the stories in *Going To Meet The Man* (1964) seem paler, less urgent and less complex. In spite of this, *Giovanni's Room* remains a powerful book because of the stark simplicity of its drama and the intensity of its vision. It deals, in the end, with the same subject as *Go Tell It On The Mountain*. Indeed, it is difficult to think of two books which deal with this subject with the same level of seriousness and urgency. The subject is the flesh itself and sexual longing, and how close to treachery lies desire, how the truth of the body differs from the lies of the mind. Like other gay writers, Baldwin could take nothing for granted. Sexual desire itself led him to being told that he should burn his book, the colour of his skin having created an original need to watch every word. His intelligence, the energy of his wit and his longing

for love hit up against history and the hardness of the
world, hit up against the prejudices which people had
about a man who was black and a man who was gay.
Everything in his fiction is bathed in the sadness
which resulted.

His religious background and his own sexuality gave
him the flesh and the devil as a great subject. Also, his
position as the eldest of his family, the surrogate father
to his siblings, his position as the outsider – the writer,
the homosexual, the one with the missing father – all
this may explain his other great subject: the extraordinary intensity in the love between siblings in his
work. This love in his fiction is all the more fierce and
concentrated because it involves the sibling as witness
to the other's self-destruction, the other's pain.

In an interview in 1970 he said:

> My family saved me . . . I mean that they kept me so
> busy caring for them, keeping them from the rats,
> roaches, falling plaster, and all the banality of poverty
> that I had no time to go jumping off the roof, or to
> become a junkie or an alcoholic. It's either/or in the
> ghetto . . . The welfare of my family has always driven
> me, always controlled me. I wanted to become rich
> and famous so no one could ever evict my family again
> . . . The greatest things in my life are my brothers and
> sisters, and my nieces and nephews.

From his first story 'The Rockpile', in which the
brothers John and Roy appear, to *Go Tell It On The
Mountain*, from the story 'Sonny's Blues' to *Tell Me*

How Long The Train's Been Gone, the love between brothers in Baldwin is elemental, like a Greek tragedy in its sense of foreboding, like 'the cup of trembling' at the end of 'Sonny's Blues', where one brother is weak and the other strong enough merely to suffer the powerlessness of one who is forced to watch. Thus Caleb in *Tell Me How Long The Train's Been Gone* is doomed, but the drama enacted in the novel is the drama of his doom as witnessed by his younger brother, the narrator, who feels for him an attachment which is fiercer than love because it knows that loss and the possibility of a tragic fate are included in the bargain. So too in *Another Country*, Ida, one of Baldwin's greatest creations, enters the novel, as Antigone enters the play, because of her love for her brother Rufus. She, too, becomes a witness to his doom. The piercing emotion surrounding family attachment in Baldwin's fiction is overwhelming; it is something so deeply felt and, in much of the fiction (including books which fail in other ways), so carefully manipulated and controlled that it is central to the achievement of his fiction, one of the reasons why he continues to be read with such intensity.

Soon after the publication of *Giovanni's Room* in 1957, James Baldwin travelled to the South to write about race. In the winter of 1959 his essay 'Nobody Knows My Name' appeared in the *Partisan Review*. 'In the fall of last year,' he wrote, my plane hovered over the rust-red earth of Georgia. I was past thirty, and I had never seen this land before. I pressed my face against the window, watching the earth come closer; soon we were just above the tops of trees. I could not suppress the thought that this earth had acquired its colour from the blood that had dripped down from these trees. My mind was filled with the image of a black man, younger than I, perhaps, or my own age, hanging from a tree, while white men watched and cut his sex from him with a knife.

Baldwin had written that his influences included 'something ironic and violent and perpetually understated in Negro speech'. Now the irony and the understatement were all gone; there was just the violence and some melodrama and a genuine sense of grief and fear and foreboding. Charlotte in North Carolina, 'a town of 165,000, was in a ferment when I was there because, of its 50,000 Negroes, four had been assigned to previously all-white schools, one to each school.' Baldwin moved in the essays of these years between the language of reportage and the language of the novelist and the preacher:

It was on the outskirts of Atlanta that I first felt how the Southern landscape – the trees, the silence, the liquid heat, and the fact that one always seems to be travelling great distances – seems designed for violence, seems, almost to demand it. What passions cannot be unleashed on a dark road on a Southern night! Everything seems so sensual, so languid, and so private. Desire can be acted out here; over this fence, behind that tree, in the darkness, there; and no one will see, no one will ever know. Only the night is watching and the night was made for desire.

It is important to imagine the impact this first journey had on Baldwin, the terror he felt and the dread, and the sense too that, no matter how freely he lived in Paris and New York, his destiny and the destiny of his country was being worked out in bitter dramatic confrontation in the South. Something in his own personality, a crucial aspect of his own talent for the darkly dramatic and the histrionic, met its match in the South.

As a novelist, he should have turned and run, because a large amount of serious imaginative energy was about to be taken up by the Civil Rights Movement over ten years and more. Baldwin never again wrote a fully successful novel. There may have been other reasons for that: the fame and money which his early writing brought him allowed him to spend time in places other than a solitary room. Also, he experimented with form in his next novel *Another Country* (1962) by killing off his main character after eighty pages. This work bears all the marks of a book written sporadically over a long period of time in many different places. The novel begins by showing us Baldwin the novelist at his most focused and intense, and it ends by suggesting that his mind was elsewhere.

It is easy to feel that he should have gone back to Paris and spent the rest of his life creating fictions in a peaceful environment, that he should have followed events as they unfolded by reading about them in the *Herald Tribune* while sipping a drink at the Deux Magots. Richard Wright remained in Paris. Neither Ralph Ellison nor Langston Hughes took part in the Civil Rights Movement (and Ellison took a dim view of Baldwin's involvement), just as writers like Brian Friel and Seamus Heaney avoided active involvement in the public life of Northern Ireland after 1972. ('Forgive my timid, circumspect involvement,' Heaney was later to write.) But Baldwin's imagination remained passionately connected to the world of his family and the destiny of his country. He lacked guile and watchfulness; the ruthlessness he had displayed in going to live in Paris and publishing *Giovanni's Room* was no use to him now. It was inevitable that someone with his curiosity and moral seriousness would want to become involved; and inevitable that someone with his sensitivity and temperament would find what was happening all-absorbing and frightening and, finally, disabling.

Baldwin's passionate involvement in the Civil Rights Movement did not make him feel at home and easy among his own people. The Civil Rights Movement was even more hostile to homosexuals than the wider society. Among the leaders of the movement there were two men who were clearly (as opposed to openly) gay. One was Baldwin; the other was Bayard Rustin. Rustin, who was more than ten years older than Baldwin, was a communist until 1941 and thereafter became a Quaker. In the war, he was imprisoned as a conscientious objector. As early as 1942 he was beaten up by the police for refusing to comply with segregation laws. He served twenty-two days on a chain gang in North Carolina in 1947 for his part in the first Freedom Ride organised by CORE and wrote a graphic and chilling account of the experience. Altogether, he was arrested twenty-four times. He adhered always to the principle of non-violence and this brought him close to Martin Luther King. He was well-read and funny and King came to enjoy his company. He had helped organise the Montgomery bus boycott in 1955.

In 1960, as Martin Luther King threatened to picket the Democratic Convention, he was threatened in turn by Adam Clayton Powell, the black congressman for Harlem, that if King didn't call off the picket, Powell would tell the press that he was having an affair with Rustin. Rustin was at that time King's special assistant and director of the New York Office of the Southern Christian Leadership Conference. King did not stand up for Rustin, he responded by distancing himself from Rustin until Rustin resigned.

Three years later when Rustin was deputy-director of the March on Washington, he was denounced in the Senate by Strom Thurmond for being a communist, a draft dodger and a homosexual. Thurmond inserted a copy of Rustin's police booking in the 1950s for indecent behaviour with other men into the Senate record. Before the March on Washington, when the FBI put a wire tap on Martin Luther King, they heard the following conversation. Someone said, 'I hope Bayard don't take a drink before the march' and Dr King replied: 'Yes, and grab one little brother. 'Cause he will grab one when he has a drink.' Rustin received much of the credit for the success of the March on Washington. In *Pillars of Fire: America in the King Years 1963–1965*, Taylor Branch wrote: 'Overnight, Rustin became if not a household name at least a quotable and respectable source for racial journalism, his former defects as a vagabond ex-communist homosexual overlooked or forgotten.' But his former defects continued to interest both King, who was worried about the damage they could to the movement, and the FBI.

The extensive FBI file on James Baldwin included the sentence: 'It has been heard that Baldwin may be a homosexual and he appeared as if he may be one.' Neither Rustin nor Baldwin was invited to speak at the end of the March on Washington. Religious elements in the movement were deeply suspicious of them. While Martin Luther King was not personally bothered by Rustin's homosexuality, some of his colleagues were. One of King's colleagues, Stanley Levinson, suggested that Baldwin and Bayard 'were better qualified to lead a homosexual movement than a civil rights movement'.

In these few years, from his famously stormy and emotional meeting with Robert Kennedy in May 1963 and his appearing on the cover of *Time* magazine the next day, Baldwin gave lectures and made speeches and went on television and travelled and organised boycotts. He wrote almost nothing. The one play and one story he wrote both seem to have been written in the white heat of the violence and fierce debate of those years. He was not writing the protest work for which he had attacked Richard Wright; he was going further. His work was directly political and, in the case of the story 'Going To Meet The Man' almost inflammatory. It is written from the point of view of a white sheriff who in the first lines of the story makes his sexual interest in black women clear, and then goes on to muse on the black boy he has arrested, and the lynching, described in lengthy and unbearable detail, which his father took him to when he was a child. Thinking of the lynching excites him and he wakes his wife and says: 'Come on, sugar, I'm going to do you like a nigger, just like a nigger, come on, sugar, and love me like you'd love a nigger.'

The story contained everything that Baldwin had so passionately preached against; it offered us the sheriff's humanity as a pure racial cliché, a demonstration of Baldwin's views on race and sex and the South and violence, without any of the subtlety of those views. Clearly, this was not a time for Jamesian distance from the burning world.

In this world, Baldwin himself was under pressure. He was not a Civil Rights strategist, such as Bayard Rustin, in daily contact with the organisation. He did not have roots in any special faction. And slowly, the brotherhood was absorbing the implications not only of *Giovanni's Room*, but also of *Another Country*, which had been a best-seller, and had shown Rufus, its black hero, as violent and self-destructive, and in the words of the Black Panther leader Eldridge Cleaver, 'a pathetic wretch who indulged in the white man's pastime of committing suicide, who let a bisexual homosexual [sic] fuck him in the ass, and who took a Southern Jezebel for his woman.'

For the young men who were ready to join the Black Panthers, Baldwin as much as Martin Luther King was part of the problem, Eldridge Cleaver, in *Soul on Ice*, published in 1968, had no difficulty identifying Baldwin's problem:

It seems that many Negro homosexuals . . . are outraged and frustrated because in their sickness they are unable to have a baby by a white man. The cross they have to bear is that, already bending over and touching their toes for the white man, the fruit of their miscegenation is not the little half-white offspring of their dreams but an increase in the unwinding of their nerves – though they redouble their efforts and intake of the white man's sperm.

Having praised Richard Wright and Norman Mailer, Cleaver wrote:

I, for one, do not think homosexuality is the latest advance over heterosexuality on the scale of human evolution. Homosexuality is a sickness, just as are baby-rape or wanting to become the head of General Motors.

The language and tone of *Going To Meet The Man* and *Soul on Ice* are part of the frenzy of the time. Baldwin and Cleaver were merely two of the many raised voices. The surprising thing is how warmly and wisely Baldwin wrote about Cleaver in *No Name In The Street*, written between 1967 and 1971:

> I was very much impressed by Eldridge . . . I knew he'd written about me in *Soul on Ice*, but I hadn't yet read it. Naturally, when I did read it, I didn't like what he had to say about me at all. But, eventually – especially as I admired the book and felt him to be valuable and rare – I thought I could see why he felt impelled to issue what was in fact a warning: he was being a zealous watchman on the city wall, and I do not say that with a sneer. He seemed to feel that I was a dangerously odd, badly twisted, and fragile reed, of too much use to the Establishment to be trusted by blacks . . . Well, I certainly hope I know more about myself, and the intention of my work than that, but I *am* an odd quantity. So is Eldridge; so are we all.

However, in an interview with the *Paris Review* in 1984, Baldwin said, 'my real difficulty with Cleaver, sadly, was visited on me by the kids who were following him, while he was calling me a faggot and the rest of it.'

Nonetheless, Baldwin became friends with various members of the Black Panthers. And part of the reason for his refusal to trade insults with Eldridge Cleaver may be that from the late 1960s Baldwin lived mostly in Istanbul or St Paul-de-Vence where he bought a large house on ten acres. Much of *No Name in the Street* was written away from the struggle, and this may explain the tolerance, if not the rambling and undisciplined tone.

In the autumn of 1960, while James Baldwin was working on *Another Country*, William Styron invited Baldwin to move into the cottage beside his house in Connecticut. Baldwin, as Styron later wrote, was the grandson of a slave; Styron was the grandson of a slave owner. Obviously, there was a great deal to discuss.

> Night after night, Jimmy and I talked, drinking whisky through the hours until the chill dawn, and I understood that I was in the company of as marvellous an intelligence as I was ever likely to encounter . . . Jimmy was a social animal of nearly manic gusto and there were some loud and festive times.

When Styron's white liberal friends expressed incredulity when Baldwin told them what was going to happen, 'Jimmy's face would become a mask of imperturbable certitude. 'Baby,' he would say softly and glare back with vast glowering eyes, 'yes, baby. I mean *burn*. We will *burn your cities down*.'

Both Baldwin and Styron agreed 'that the writer should be free to demolish the barrier of colour, to cross the forbidden line and write from the point of view of someone with a different skin.' Baldwin had already published *Giovanni's Room*; now it was Styron's turn. When in 1967 he published *The Confessions of Nat Turner*, which was written in the first person, using the voice of a black slave, and was greeted with rage and indignation by most black writers and intellectuals, Baldwin supported him. His statement – 'He has begun the common history – *ours*' – was unlikely to have made Baldwin any friends among the Black Panthers.

Baldwin remained independent in these difficult years, toeing no party line. Although during his time in America in the 1960s there were long nights spent drinking whisky and 'being a social animal of nearly manic gusto', what he remembered most from those years were the murders of people he knew, people he had marched with and worked with. These years for him were punctuated not as much by the publication of his books as by the terrible toll which those who led the movement had to pay. The long period of dullness and quietness required to write a novel had no chance against the heart-breaking urgency of the daily news. Not long after the assassination of Martin Luther King, Baldwin was sent the proofs of *Tell Me How Long The Train's Been Gone*, but failed to return them, according to James Campbell in *Talking at the Gates: A Life of James Baldwin*. When the head of the Dial Press went to Baldwin's house to discuss changes, 'Jimmy said, "Do what you like".'

Baldwin spent much of the last twenty years of his life in France, where he died in 1987 with his brother David and Lucien Happersberger, whom he had known for almost forty years, at his bedside. 'To save myself,' he told an interviewer in 1970, 'I finally had to leave for good . . . One makes decisions in funny ways; you make a decision without knowing you've made it. I suppose my decision was made when Malcolm X was killed, when Martin Luther King was killed, when Medgar Evans and John and Bobby and Fred Hampton were killed. I loved Medgar. I loved Martin and Malcolm. We all worked together and kept the faith together. Now they are all dead. When you think about it, it is incredible. I'm the last witness – everybody else is dead. I couldn't stay in America. I had to leave.'

In the end, he was not a political thinker, or even a novelist like Styron or Mailer whose works were fired by politics. He was interested in the soul's dark intimate spaces much more than in the body politic. He was closer as an artist to Ingmar Bergman, whom he admired and wrote about, than to any of his American contemporaries. His essays are riveting because he insists on being personal, on forcing the public and the political to submit to his voice and the test of his experience and his observation. He was interested in the self, in the hidden and dramatic areas in his own being, and was prepared to explore difficult truths about his own core self in his fiction. Because he was black, he had to battle in his fiction for the right of his protagonists to choose, or half-choose, their destinies. He knew about guilt and rage and bitter privacies in a way that none of his American novelist contemporaries did. And this was not simply because he was black and homosexual, it arose also from the very nature of his talent, from the tone of his sensibility. 'All art,' he wrote, 'is a kind of confession, more or less oblique. All artists, if they are to survive, are forced, at last, to tell the whole story, to vomit the anguish up.'

THOM GUNN:

THE ENERGY OF THE PRESENT

'F AME IS DIFFICULT FOR A WRITER TO DEAL WITH,'
Thom Gunn writes in his essay on Allen
Ginsberg's poetry.

> It dries you up, or it makes you think you are infall-
> ible, or your writing becomes puffed out with
> self-esteem. (Victor Hugo thought himself superior to
> both Jesus and Shakespeare.) It is a complication that
> the imagination can well do without.

It is the spring of 1993. Gunn is on the list of those
who will read at a literary festival in a huge old
market building in the centre of San Francisco,
which has been his home town since the late Fifties.
His first book in eleven years, *The Man with Night
Sweats*, has just been published. The main auditorium holds thousands who are here to see their
favourite writers. People sit on the floor because all
the chairs are taken up. All eyes are on Armistead
Maupin as he reads from his new book and answers
questions about sexual politics. Crowds stare in

wonder as Isabel Allende reads from a new novel. After her reading she will sit at a table in a side stall and sign copies of her books. The queue to get her signature stretches into the next stall, where Thom Gunn is due to read, so we have to wait. There are maybe thirty or forty of us. In the distance we can hear the voice of another main attraction holding the crowd in the central auditorium.

I am surprised that Gunn is not a main attraction. I thought that those early tough poems delighting in the body's toughness ('Much that is natural, to the will must yield'), the urge to write memorable lines ('Are you a warning, Father, or an example?'), the fascination with low life and moral ambiguity ('Oh dead punk lady with the knack/Of looking fierce in pins and black,/The suburbs wouldn't want you back'), and the frank versions of a gay overworld ('Yet when I've had you once or twice/I may not want you any more') would have made him a guru here; I presumed that his recent elegies on the deaths of friends from AIDS would have made him a central figure in the literary life of San Francisco.

But much of his poetry has also been laden down with paradox and wit; it is deeply conscious of several great traditions. 'The care and the cunning of the style,' as he has written of Yeats's 'In Memory of Major Robert Gregory', 'its very finish', serves 'to place all impulsive decisions many drafts anterior to the version we read.' There is a beautiful neutrality, most of the time, in his tone. He gives nothing away. He does not know, just as the reader must not know, how much of his secret self is in the poems. In *The Occasions of Poetry*, a book of essays, he writes about his poem 'From an Asian Tent':

> What does it do if I say . . . that in it I am finally able to write about my father? . . . I would like the poem read as being about what it proclaims as its subject: Alexander the Great remembering Philip of Macedon.

The middle stanza of 'From an Asian Tent' reads:

> *You held me once before the army's eyes;*
> *During their endless shout, I tired and slid*
> *Down past your forearms to the cold surprise*
> *Your plated shoulder made between my thighs.*
> *This happened. Or perhaps I wish it did.*

Anyone reading this will know, from the tone, that the poem is not, on the one hand, an exercise or a mere exploration of a historical moment, nor, on the other hand, a simple study in autobiography. The feeling in the poem is too real and exact to be explained away by whim, or, indeed, experience. 'The poem's truth is in its faithfulness to a possibly imagined feeling, not to my history,' Gunn writes.

Gunn's history is contained in his *Collected Poems*, which includes work published between 1954 and 1992. Any gay reader looking at those dates will know that something momentous for gay people – the breaking of the silence – happened between those years. This makes Gunn's work especially important for gay readers.

Gunn's work is, however, also interesting for every reader. During those years he is an English poet partly becoming an American poet, a poet steeped in the rhythms of the sixteenth century in England basking in the glories of the twentieth century in California, and a poet nurtured on the iambic pentameter sometimes playing with more free forms. But he is also in the Fifties and Sixties a gay poet finding strategies to expose and disguise his own sexuality. It is tempting to read 'Carnal Knowledge', for example, as simply about a gay man in bed with a woman:

> *I am not what I seem, believe me, so*
> *For the magnanimous pagan I pretend*
> *Substitute a forked creature as your friend.*
> *When darkness lies without a roll or stir*
> *Flaccid, you want a competent poseur.*
> *I know you know I know you know I know.*

'The danger of biography, and equally of autobiography,' Gunn has written

is that it can muddy poetry by confusing it with its sources . . . In my early twenties I wrote a poem called 'Carnal Knowledge', addressed to a girl, with a refrain making variations on the phrase 'I know you know'. Now anyone aware that I am homosexual is likely to misread the whole poem, inferring that the thing 'known' is that the speaker would prefer to be in bed with a man. But that would be a serious misreading, or at least a serious misplacement of emphasis. The poem, actually addressed to a fusion of two completely different girls, is not saying anything as clear-cut as that. A reader knowing nothing about the author has a much better chance of understanding it.

The reader who knows that Gunn is gay is likely also to view the tone of restraint and neutrality in his work as aspects of a mask he invented as a gay man in the Fifties. And this may represent a serious misreading of his work. Other readers can argue that whether he is gay or straight makes no difference, that there is no such thing as a 'gay poem', there is only good poetry and bad poetry. Yet a gay reader is likely to read Gunn's *Collected Poems* in a different way from a straight reader. Gunn, in an interview with Tony Sarver, helps explain why this is the case. When he asked if the Gay Movement had helped him as a writer, he said:

> Yes, very much I think. In my early books I was in the closet. I was discreet in an Audenish way. If a poem referred to a lover, I always used 'you'. I figured it didn't matter, it didn't affect the poetry. But it did. Later I came out, and Ian Young included me in his Male Muse anthology, so that I'd officially gone public. Now, I wouldn't have expected it to make so much difference as it did. In the title poem of 'Jack Straw's Castle' [written between 1973 and 1974] I end up in bed with a man, and I wrote this quite naturally, without a second thought. Ten years ago, I

doubt if the incident would have appeared in the poem. It wouldn't have occurred to me to end in that way.

The world from Shakespeare to contemporary advertising has been so full of images of heterosexuality that no one notices, but these images are nonetheless absorbed into the most secret and private part of the self. This hidden part of the gay self remains hungry for such ratifying images; it most fully recognises this need when the need is satisfied, the silence broken, the words spelled out 'quite naturally, without a second thought.' Gunn's *Collected Poems* enacts the experience of many gay men all over the Western world. In the tone of those sixteenth-century poems which have been important for Gunn, such as Sir Thomas Wyatt's elegies on the death of friends, there is a sense of restriction about what can and cannot be said, and that restriction offers the poem a tension and an inner drama. Gunn's early work strives for a neutral, almost impersonal tone; in this work there is a respect for restriction. I love what's hidden between the lines of these early poems. But then watching Gunn describe, with a freedom which is quite new, what it is like to be in bed with another man in, say, 'Jack Straw's Castle' is, from the gay point of view, like being there for the Annunciation:

> So humid, we lie sheetless – bare and close,
> Facing apart, but leaning ass to ass.
> And that mere contact is sufficient touch,

A hinge, it separates but not too much.
An air moves over us, as calm and cool
As the green water of a swimming pool.

What if this is the man I gave my key
Who got in while I slept? or what if he,
Still, is a dream of the same man?
No, real.
Comes from outside the castle, I can feel.
The beauty's in what is, not what may seem.
I turn. And even if he were a dream
– Thick sweating flesh against which I lie curled –
With dreams like this, Jack's ready for the world.

Thom Gunn on the platform is warm and affable, but he maintains a somewhat distant air. He is not in love with his own voice; some of his mind is elsewhere; he will not detain us longer than is necessary. His voice is calm. In a time when poets have held on tight to their focus and tone, Gunn has been concerned with contradictions. He has studied under two rigid and dogmatic teachers, F.R. Leavis and Yvor Winters, and yet he remains open to things, almost casual in his opposition to the notion of dogma.

At the end there is time for questions. Always you want to know how poems came, and always, too, a poet like Gunn must resist answering, he must leave the mystery to its own devices. 'I borrow heavily from my reading,' he has written, 'because I take my reading seriously: it is part of my total experience and I base most of my poetry on my experience.' There are things about his reading and his writing that I would love to know. I find myself suddenly eager with my hand up ready to ask a question.

'Fifteen years ago,' he wrote in 1966, 'the English hardly credited North America with having any poetry at all; but they are now, it turns out, ready to accept all and any American poetry.' In an interview, published at the end of *Shelf Life*, his collection of essays and criticism, he mentions that 'the English' don't think that his free verse is very good. 'I don't think that they can hear free verse, actually,' the interviewer says. 'I don't think they can hear it either,' Gunn replies. He mentions that he chose to publish a pamphlet of free verse in England. 'Just to irritate them?' the interviewer asks. 'Just to irritate them,' Gunn assents.

In his two books of criticism he has been concerned to explain and read the American free verse tradition, to try and cure even the most Irish of us of our Englishness. In *The Occasions of Poetry* there are essays on Williams, Snyder and Robert Duncan, and in *Shelf Life* on Whitman, H.D., Marianne Moore, Mina Loy, Robert Creeley, Allen Ginsberg and two essays on Robert Duncan. He reprints his review of Helen Vendler's book of contemporary poetry (published by Harvard in the US and by Faber in Britain), 'an obviously worthless book', for him, because it narrows the ground of American poetry, excluding the two extremes of Charles Olson ('the poet who actually *feared* closure, each rhyme an exclusion') and J.V.

Cunningham ('who saw language as the mark of human choice, each phrase a closure, each rhyme an exclusion'). It is clear from his own poetry and from his criticism that he is only too ready to read both and argue the case for both, and for others who have been left out of the canon, rather than join in the fashionable argument between the New Formalists and the Language Poets.

He is excited by the idea in Robert Duncan's work of 'an open poetry in which the process of writing gets excitingly out of control, thus admitting interesting accidents and unforeseen directions'. Duncan, he writes, 'believes in the centrality of what we call accident or chance. By our inadvertence and error we find out what we really mean, beyond and beneath purpose . . . Everything depends on the energy of the present.' At this stage, it is hard not to wish that Yvor Winters, or even F.R. Leavis, would come in to break all this up. But the essays on Duncan help us to engage with some of those poems by Gunn – 'The Geysers', 'Wrestling' (dedicated to Duncan) and 'The Menace' – which, for those of us brought up on the idea of poetry as ironic and formal and worked-on, are hard to read. 'Wrestling' begins:

Discourse
of sun and moon
fire and beginnings
behind words
the illuminated words

My problem here is that I am not sure what Gunn is talking about. I am not even English but I still want a verb. I don't know why I go back to these poems so often; maybe it is because I admire the poems which surround them so much; maybe there is another reason, something compelling in their verblessness, which I don't yet know. Is he writing down anything that comes into his head? This is essentially what he recommends about Duncan's procedures. For someone as steeped in the sound of the iambic pentameter line and the syllabic form as Gunn was, the freedom of free verse and aleatory writing must have offered great release, like learning to swim in early middle age. But his own best work still seems that which is most concentrated and may have been most revised.

His work with the syllabic line, however, offered him a density and calmness of tone which produced masterpieces like 'Considering the Snail', which no other English poet nor any American poet could have written: it is open and closed at the same time, like the poem 'Touch'. I feel that these are poems that were worked on over and over in order to seem casual, easy to read and unLatinate.

Gunn had no central myth or topic to get him through a lifetime's work, as Larkin, Lowell and Hughes did and Heaney does. Instead, he pushed against his own talent for making formal, Latinate poems, to play with a language which was more relaxed and open-ended and all-American. In his essay on Allen Ginsberg he is at his most convincing, acknowledging 'the feeling around' that Ginsberg may be 'more of a *public figure* than a *poet*'; but insisting on Ginsberg's honesty and humour while acknowledging his banality and other weaknesses. He is prepared to study lines and passages closely; he finds real skill and precision in Ginsberg's language, and then reads on, mixing sense and enthusiasm in a way which is really rare, calling 'Many Loves' 'unique among erotic poems'. 'It is the rhythm and language of reverence, of awe, of sanctity without sanctimoniousness.'

Meanwhile we are back in San Francisco and I still have my hand up. I want to know when Gunn first came across certain poems, the elegies I have mentioned by Sir Thomas Wyatt for friends who were executed that weren't published until the early Sixties. They seem close in so many ways to the poems in the last section of *The Man with Night Sweats*. He referred to these poems in a book review. He obviously knows them well. Their tone is bare and full of grief: there is no room for play or fancy ornament. Did they matter to him, and did they help him to write the poems in *The Man with Night Sweats*? He is wary of the question. He thinks for a moment: he had read one of them, maybe two before he started on his own sequence, but, he goes on, influence is such a hard thing to know anything about, some things make a difference, others don't, it's hard to tell. He smiles, making clear that this is over. He wants to go.

'Enmeshed with Time', the essay on Wyatt and others, is in *Shelf Life*. Gunn quotes from 'In Mourning Wise':

And thus farewell, each one in hearty wise.
The axe is home, your heads be in the street.
The trickling tears doth fall so from mine eyes,
I scarce may write, my paper is so wet.

He comments:

The axe's work is over and their heads are on display, but the phrases employed are so mildly, almost comfortably familiar that they increase the horror of the line . . . The understated force is such that it spills over into a kind of authentification of the next two lines, making us read as simple truth an imagery that might otherwise have seemed commonplace in its overstatement.

'I scarce may write, my paper is so wet.' The line is haunting in its perfect plainness, and more powerful if you know that the dead were traitors and the poem is dangerous and would be hidden away and not found for more than four centuries. Gunn is fascinated by the dead, and if you read certain poems and essays carefully, it is easy to see that the impulse behind the poems in *The Man with Night Sweats* is there from early in his career. In his essay on Ginsberg he praises poems in which the dead return in dreams and then adds in parenthesis: 'as they do to all of us, don't they?' They may do, but in Gunn's poem 'The Reassurance', the ghostly presence and its effect seem oddly more real than anything any of us have witnessed or felt:

About ten days or so
After we saw you dead
You came back in a dream.
I'm all right now you said.

And it was *you, although*
You were fleshed out again:
You hugged us all round then,
And gave your welcoming beam.

How like you to be kind,
Seeking to reassure.
And, yes, how like my mind
To make itself secure.

This is Gunn at his most perfect and plain; the tone is like that in Yeats's 'Politics', Larkin's 'The Trees' or Elizabeth Bishop's 'Sonnet', the short poem offering a sudden moment of realisation. Gunn has always written as though he trusted rhyme and was prepared to let its fall be blunt, if necessary – as in a ballad, or a poem by Hardy. In *The Occasions of Poetry* he writes about Hardy's poems of 1913:

> He particularly records his own losses as only important because they are a part of other people's losses. It is never the poetry of personality . . . He must have been a genuinely modest man. His first person speaks as a sample human being, with little personality displayed and no claims for uniqueness.

The essay was written in 1972; now, something similar could be written about Gunn's laments for friends who died of AIDS.

He writes in detail in *Shelf Life* about Robert Creeley's poem 'The World', in which a man in bed with his sleeping wife sees the ghost of her dead brother: 'I wanted so ably/to reassure you,' the poem begins.

> *I tried to say, it is*
> *all right, she is*
> *happy, you are no longer*

> *needed.*

Gunn comes to us as a poet first, alert to tradition and craft, studious and concerned with form. It would be easy to claim that what he did with his talent, opening it to the energy of the present, searching for looser and more relaxed forms, arose from his search as a gay man for a more relaxed way to live, a place with looser rules. On the other hand, this may simply not be true. It may be that the generosity of his work as a critic, and indeed as a poet, arises from the generosity of his spirit and this can be placed besides his homosexuality, as another aspect of him, rather than claimed as an attribute of his gay self.

It is also possible that Gunn's poems written in a more relaxed form took their bearings from his own liberation won in California in the Seventies, and that the elegiac voice of his masterpieces in *The Man with*

Night Sweats, which is direct, unmasked and personal, arose from the battle he won to speak freely. Yet poets from Wyatt to Hardy have found this tone before, hurt into using it by circumstances which are similar to those suffered by Gunn, which do not depend on homosexuality. Gunn's homosexuality has clearly guided his work; despite our urge as gay readers to ask his poems to touch our hidden spirit, which has been unspeakable for so many centuries, we must acknowledge that his talent, his seriousness, his intelligence and his generosity, if they can be separated from it, have been as important as his homosexuality in the making of his poems.

Shelf Life: Essays, Memoirs and an Interview by Thom Gunn, Faber

The Occasions of Poetry by Thom Gunn, Faber

Collected Poems by Thom Gunn, Faber

PEDRO ALMODÓVAR:

THE LAWS OF DESIRE

MADRID, FOR PEDRO ALMODÓVAR, IS STILL A PLACE
of mystery and glamour and excitement. But
when he walks the streets now, everybody wants to
have their photograph taken with him, or video him,
or have him sign an autograph. We are standing waiting to pay after a lunch at an outdoor café and he is
impatient. One part of him dislikes it, wishes he could
be more anonymous in the city he spent his childhood
dreaming about. Someone has been videoing him as
he was eating and now someone else, who can't
believe her luck, comes up asking for an autograph.
Pedro looks glum, and wants to get this over with,
briskly taking a pen and a piece of paper. And then
something happens, as it always does. He catches the
eye of his fan, or he makes a remark, and every time
it is the same, his face breaks open, he starts to joke
and laugh, he starts to perform, he wants to please
others and amuse himself. It is as though he has a new
friend. The Almódovar who just one minute ago
wanted peace and privacy has gone indoors.

He spends a lot of time indoors these days in his

apartment near the centre of Madrid. He could not imagine writing in the countryside. He loves the city, the buzz of the streets, even when he is protected from the noise by double-glazing. This is how he writes his scripts, using the part of himself that is private, deliberate and solitary, the part of himself that no one is allowed close to, and hardly anyone knows about.

In the morning, in the café opposite his apartment, he keeps his head down, his face expressionless. He is preoccupied, he doesn't want to talk. He quietly orders a coffee. When I mention a mutual friend, a painter and performer I knew in Barcelona twenty-five years ago and he knew too, he talks about his death calmly and sadly. Our friend was a painter but, Almodóvar agrees, not a good painter; his real talent lay in decorating his face and his body, in dressing up as a senorita from Seville in elaborate and colourful dress and headgear, and walking the streets or going to festivals. Both of us knew him in the late 1970s when he was funny and outrageous, and both of us grow silent now, once Almodóvar discovers that I know how he ended. Dressed as Apollo, all in paper, our friend was at a festival where someone set him on fire and he died of the burns.

Almodóvar is one of the survivors. From the time he spent in London in the early 1970s, to the period when he hung out with the wild crowd in Madrid and Barcelona in the wild years after Franco's death, he has managed to come through. He knows that and thinks about it, and it gives him a sort of melancholy strength and solitariness to place beside his extrovert and flamboyant self and his love of the bizarre and the quirky.

In those years, he, more than any of the others, would have laughed at the idea of a country house, but that is where we are going now, to Pedro Almódovar's country house which is half an hour out of Madrid in a development which is protected by a security guard. This is where he comes to play with his family and friends. His brother Agustin, his executive producer, has two young sons who love the swimming-pool and the tennis courts and the pool table and the sense of freedom. This is a place for parties and gatherings.

From the outside the house is an ordinary piece of suburban posh, almost nondescript. But once you go inside, Almodóvar's mark, which you see in his films, is all over the house. Garish colours placed close to other garish colours, yellows and reds, amazing blues. In the kitchen the fridge and cooker are painted orange. Outlandish objects or ordinary ornaments or pieces of kitsch are gathered together as though they were prized collectors' items. The house itself is a form of entertainment. Over one door there are versions of the crucifixion beside sunbursts in various styles. Every object seems chosen for its craziness. This is the public Almodóvar, the party-goer who clearly loved placing the yellow-framed photographs of family and friends in the hallway carefully askew. Nothing is symmetrical in his world.

The back of the house gives on to bare fields, the

dry, washed colours of Castile with the sierra in the distance. He likes the privacy here, but nature puzzles him, bores him. He likes the garden, but doesn't tend it himself. I like to have it, he says, but I don't communicate with flowers. He grins to himself at such an unlikely idea. He enjoys playing the host, putting on loud music, making jokes. In his bedroom, he looks in the mirror and makes faces at himself. He is trying to lose weight, he says. (This doesn't prevent him from ordering fried eggs and fried potatoes the next day.) He narrows his eyes at the mirror and grins in mock despair. He doesn't like his face, he says. He examines himself carefully. His face is amazingly flexible and lived in. He frowns at himself and gives a magnificent shrug before getting ready to go downstairs.

In his work he plays with opposites and doubles and secret identities. So now when he struts out of the house in his tennis gear, you know that one more of his own hidden identities has just appeared. He is all business. His face is serious, his expression set. This time he looks like a guy who would lead a heavy-duty marketing drive, or a leader who could turn the economy around. You don't mess with Pedro Almodóvar in tennis gear.

When he starts to play, it is clear that he has no style, there is nothing flamboyant about the way he moves and responds. But even when he's fooling around on the court, he's serious and determined. He doesn't want to waste time; he is competitive, he suggests we get down to business and play the best of three. He likes things to be structured. His opponents call him

The Wall because he will hit anything back. Playing against him, he says with pride, is like Chinese water torture. He doesn't hit winners, and he doesn't place the ball with any great skill, but he takes enormous care to make no mistakes. He returns almost everything. He is oddly awkward, but in deadly earnest. He is all stamina and brute strength. And if you hit a winner down the side, he doesn't look disappointed or hurt but goes and gets the ball and starts again. Nothing fazes him or frightens him. If you were asked to judge his character on the basis of his game, you would say that he is cautious and consistent, almost boring; he takes no risks, he is a plodder, you could think, a worker, dull and methodical. After a few games, you could confidently make him your account-ant, your project manager.

He was the little boy who couldn't stop singing. Brought up in provincial Spain, born in 1951 into a world he describes as isolated, austere and sober, he remembers the images of the Virgin and the crucifix over the bed and some photographs of family as the only decorations in the house. At the age of ten he was a star in school. At night when all the other boys on the dormitory were undressing, getting ready for bed, his job was to read them the Lives of the Saints, gruesome, bloody and action-packed stories as he remembers, and he is deeply alert to the peculiar, raw sensuality of the scene. He read the stories of the martyrs and saints with the same relish as he did the adventure stories he also read aloud to the whole school from a podium during meal times. He was the only one chosen to read like this. He loved the Gregorian chants, singing the Latin mass, he loved anything that involved performance. But he did not like the priests and he did not like his religious education.

His rebellion began in adolescence. His contact with the outside world came from the radio and pop magazines. In a world that was fearful and conformist, his long hair caused consternation. He wanted to go to the city, but his father found him a job in a bank. In Spain in those years, if you found a job, you took it and kept it and viewed yourself lucky. That battle with his father is still vivid for him. He didn't understand me, he says, he didn't know how to use his authority. But Pedro Almodóvar was absolutely sure what he had to do: he had to go to Madrid, and he knew even then that he wanted to make films.

He is still basking in the sheer joy of those early years in Madrid. There was a singer he came across then, on record and on the radio; he knew she lived in the city, and there was something about her gravelly voice, a raw, melodramatic energy, a sense of pain and hurt and infinite loss, that he wanted badly. Her singing was self-exposure, her expression a form of healing or redemption and he loved the idea of that. The sheer force of her pride and solitude and sadness meant everything to this adolescent boy new in the city. The singer's name was Chavela Vargas and Pedro went everywhere in search of her, he asked everybody where she was, but she had gone. Yes, she had been in the city but there was no trace of her now. Haunted by her songs, he kept looking but she had disappeared.

In the late 1960s in Madrid and Barcelona, young people behaved as though Franco, dictator since the end of the Civil War in 1939, were already dead, although he did not officially die until 1975. Nonetheless, Franco managed to close the film school just as Almodóvar wanted to go there, thus forcing him to teach himself and forge his own style. Pedro hung around with the hippies and the purveyors of counter-culture in the Plaza Santa Ana and the streets around it. He went to every film he could. He wrote poetry and stories and he got to know people from the theatre. 'I am,' he says, 'still in recovery from that time.'

But there are two stories he tells that show other aspects of him, that illustrate his essential toughness and determination, stubbornness, self-discipline and will to survive. Not to speak of his charm. Military service in Spain in those years was the bane of everyone's life. Just as you had fallen in love, or just as you had fallen in with the hip crowd, you would be dragged off for a vicious hair-cut and made to spend a year in the army. Everyone loathed it, but Almodóvar's response to it was particularly intense.

He describes it as an absolute nightmare, and his reaction was to build a crust around himself, programme himself and prepare himself. He did not speak once to anyone for twelve months. The little boy who had been the priests' favourite and was popular among his fellows, the adolescent who had managed to make peace with his parents and find a whole world of friendship in Madrid, decided that he did not want anyone to know him. Not just the officers, but the other boys doing military service. He ignored everyone. He read Proust, he says. And he listened with distaste to the conversations about sex on the dormitory. 'All rites interest me,' he says, 'especially the Catholic ceremonies as theatre, but the military doesn't.' He has no friends from that time.

In Madrid he worked at various jobs, but eventually he did exams and an interview for a job in the national telephone company. For the interview, he managed to disguise his long hair by using hair-oil and putting it in a bun, but when he arrived in his new job, no one would work with him. Long hair was still considered scandalous. There was, however, a limit to their power, he says; they couldn't just fire him for having long hair. And he enjoyed the crisis, took pleasure in watching them work out what they were going to do. He says that he did not want to scandalise anyone, but neither was he going to have his hair cut. Finally, one of them relented and agreed to work with him. Within two months, he says, he had won the rest of them over, and they all grew to love him, despite his long hair.

His job was to exchange new telephone apparatuses for old ones, and to his delight he began to meet a new breed, and they would help him make his name. He met the Spanish middle classes whom he had not known before, and he had an opportunity to study middle-class women from Madrid at a time of social change when everyone in the city was going through an identity crisis of some sort and the dictatorship was coming to an end. A new telephone apparatus was an essential element for a new self in the new Spain. The old black bakelite apparatus belonged to the dark ages.

He bought a Super-8 camera with his first pay-cheque, and he showed his films wherever he could. His work was different: he told stories while others made vague, arty and conceptual films. From the minute he began, no matter how small the venue, he could make people roar with laughter. Among the Super-8 people, he stood out as too populist, but once he began to make full-length films – and he made his first one while still working in the telephone company – he stood out from the other Spanish film-makers who were obsessed with the Civil War. His civil war had been with his father, and what he saw around him was too interesting, Madrid on the verge of a nervous breakdown. When he finally left the telephone company, they told him that they would hold his job for him in case he ever needed it again.

Elena Benarroch is the woman who has made the fur coat fashionable again in Spain and she has the look, as she stands in the hallway of her apartment near the centre of Madrid, of a serious party-giver. Her living room is a party-giver's dream, and her guest-list tonight is going to make the society columns of all the Spanish newspapers; the society magazine *¡Hola!* will devote two pages to it.

The party is for the designer Jean-Paul Gaultier, but the party is also an excuse for mixing all the elements that make up Madrid and seeing what will happen. Former Socialist Prime Minister Felipe Gonzalez is here with his wife Carmen Romero, as is General Franco's granddaughter Carmen Martinez-Bordiu. Almodóvar is here, and many other from Spanish film. The room is coming down with actors and models. Someone points out the latest star of Spanish television and a beautiful young man fresh in from Cuba. As a long-standing devotee of *¡Hola!* I know for sure that I am in my element when I see a certain woman coming into the room. She is called Isabel Preysler, and she is the most famous woman in Spain. Part of her mystery and allure is that she is not an actress or a performer, that she is best known from the society pages and the covers of magazines. Everyone in Spain will be able to list her husbands: first, the singer Julio Iglesias; second, the Marquis de Grinon; now the politician Miguel Boyer.

As she floats through the crowd, everyone watches her, checks out how smooth and clear her skin is, how young she looks, and how oddly disengaged she appears from things, how fragile she seems. The party is hotting up.

Every time I look for Almodóvar, I find him talking to the same woman, sometimes the conversation between them is filled with laughter, but once I look over and he is back in his business-like, dead serious mode and both he and his woman friend are locked in some grave, deep conversation, as though they are hearing each other's confessions or discussing their tax returns. The woman could be in her seventies, she is short, her hair is grey and cut close, her skin is nut brown, her eyes are the most alert and alive in the room. The aura around her is one of immense sadness and immense power.

I know who she is, because earlier in the day Pedro has told me the story. She is Chavela Vargas, the woman whose voice haunted him when he was a kid, the woman he searched for when he first came to Madrid. She gave up singing for twenty-five years during which she lived it up and lived it down in Mexico. ('There is no good tequila in Mexico any-more,' Pedro says. 'Chavela drank it all.') And then the woman whom Pedro calls the higher priestess of pain came back to Madrid. This was the only time, he says, when his fame was useful. He set about making Chavela famous all over again. He went with her to the smallest venues, introduced her, cajoled people to listen to her. He used her in his films *Kika* and *Flower of My Secret*. Her voice was as expressive and precise as ever. Her face, Pedro says, is the face of a primitive god. And if you go into a music shop in Madrid now you will find all her old work re-issued and all her new work on sale. She is a star.

Now she is going to sing, and Pedro is going to sing with her to start things off, and they need to create space in the crowded room. When I look around I notice that another great Spanish singer Martirio has arrived at the party with her son Raul who normally accompanies her on guitar. I settle down with a large drink near the piano. Felipe Gonzalez comes over too and sits close to the music.

Chavela's voice can move from being melancholy and breathy to becoming tobacco-stained and fierce. She sings her heart out as a group gathers around her. Some of the songs tell of an inexpressible sadness. Pedro cannot take his eyes off her. He is delighted, he loves this melodrama; sometimes he makes as though to direct her, he smiles at her and gestures, as though pulling the song out of her. Come on, he seems to suggest, more emotion, give it more. She watches him and smiles darkly, loving him back.

And then something astonishing happens. Chavela begins another song, this one even sadder than the last. If you leave me, you will ruin my world, the words tell us, and Chavela sings these words as though she means them. I can see Pedro's face clearly, and he is going to cry. He is following the words as though everything depended on them. His face is like a child's and he is listening to the song as a child will listen to a story. He is letting it enter his spirit. For days, he has been complaining to me about his own appearance, how much he hates it; in those moments as the song comes to an end, and Chavela sings out the concluding stanza ('If you leave me, I will die') he looks incredibly beautiful. As she finishes, I notice that Martirio's son, who is accompanying Chavela on the guitar, has tears in his eyes. I want this night to go on forever.

It does. By about two-thirty, everyone, led by Elena Benarroch, is brave enough to begin throwing Elena

Benarroch's red carnations at Chavela, Martirio and Raul. Everybody is calling for more. The waiters are still serving drinks. Isabel Preysler is looking even more elusive and enigmatic. Later, about an hour later, I will watch her and Chavela having a long talk that seems deeply private and intimate. I would give anything to know what they are talking about. But for now Pedro is still watching his old friend, and she is surpassing herself, shouting out her rage and passion with her arms outstretched.

In a room full of the rich and the beautiful and the powerful, he has paid no attention to anyone else all night. And now it's getting late and there are interruptions and side shows. Pedro has no patience with this. All the aspects which make up his complex personality are now on show: he wants to direct Chavela Vargas; he wants to cry; he wants to re-live his youth; he cannot stop watching this strong woman who has perfected the art of self-expression and self-invention; and he cannot handle this show being interrupted. I watch him studying the scene. I watch him realising that the best part of the night is over. I watch him deciding, just like that, what he's going to do. I watch his face change back to the serious, determined survivor who loves managing chaos, but hates it getting beyond his control. In one second, he's gone.

MARK DOTY:
THE SEARCH FOR REDEMPTION

THE WORDS 'HIV POSITIVE' AND 'AIDS' DO NOT
appear in the poems in Mark Doty's *My
Alexandria* (1995); instead, they hover in the spaces
between the other words, and they govern the tone
of almost every poem. Now, with the appearance of
Heaven's Coast: A Memoir, we know that Doty's
boyfriend Wally Roberts was dying slowly from AIDS
when these poems were being written. Doty also
kept a diary during that time, some of which he
quotes in the memoir. *Heaven's Coast* deals with
each change in Wally's illness; the book is a charting
of the mixture of the mundane and the miraculous, if
I can use that word, in the manner of Wally's dying.
Thus the poems don't need to tell the story, they
don't depend on the medical details or the days when
things happened. They seek instead, desperately, to
find images and rhythms which will make sense of
this illness, a scheme which can accommodate it,
however fitfully and sadly. They seek to describe the
world in all its wonder, as though it were the world
which were being slowly eaten away by this disease,

as though it were nature itself that would soon disappear and would not come back. In the first poem in *My Alexandria*, 'Demolition', Doty invokes the ghost of Robert Lowell: many of the poems take their bearings from Lowell's clotted diction, from what Doty calls his 'ruthless energy', from Lowell's interest in burning the poem onto the page, heaping on adjectives to fuel the fire, invoking the Old Testament; writing, if he possibly could, his own Old Testament.

Doty's is a land of plenty, his poems celebrate abundance. In the 'The Wings', he and his companion find an abandoned orchard, 'the long flattened grasses' are 'gorged' with windfalls; in the same poem.

the auctioneer holds up

now the glass lily severed
from its epergne, now the mother-of-pearl
lorgnette.

'Some days,' he writes,

things yield

such grace and complexity that what we see
seems offered.

The landscape of these poems is over-rich, almost sated, with images of redemption and beauty; the material world is for Doty 'a permanent harvest'. In another section of the same poem he and his companion see an AIDS quilt exhibited which bears 'the unthinkable catalogue of the names'; some panels display items of clothing, jeans or a shirt stitched onto the quilt:

> *One can't look past*
>
> *the sleeves where two arms*
> *were, where a shoulder pushed*
> *against a seam, and someone knew exactly*
>
> *how the stitches pressed against skin*
> *that can't be generalised but was,*
> *irretrievably, you, or yours.*

Here the voice stops oddly, almost catches, on the 'were' and the 'was'; in these poems Doty lets the pain of what is happening to him over these two or three years write itself into the structure of the lines.

At times he puts moments from the story into the poems: his own first homosexual experience in 'Days of 1981'; Wally's testing positive ('I would say anything else/in the world, any other word') in 'Fog'. But most of the time, the references to his lover's dying are oblique, buried in the text, and more powerful for that. At times it helps to know the story, to have read *Heaven's Coast* and thus know the context for a poem like 'The Ware Collection of Glass Flowers and Fruit, Harvard Museum', which ends with an image of glass-blowing as

> *an art*
> *mouthed to the shape of how soft things are,*
> *how good, before they disappear.*

To know the facts which underlie the manic melancholy of these poems, the reason for the creation of images of pure, shared, intense, private happiness and the constant search for transcendence, does not rob the poems of their mystery as much as emphasise how artful and trusting in the processes of poetry they are.

In *My Alexandria*, the garden in September is 'this ordered enactment of desire': in the first poem in *Atlantis*, Doty asks: 'What is description, after all,/but encoded desire?' And now he can equate 'the ferocity of dying' with the 'luminosity/of what's living *hardest*'. The tone here has become very much more relaxed:

> *Autumn's a grand old drag*
> *in torched and tumbled chiffon*
> *striking her weary pose.*

This is a looser music, at times almost slack. ('All afternoon the town readied for storm,/men in the harbour shallows hauling in small boats/that rise and fall on the tide.') The echoes of early Lowell and Keats and the Old Testament have given way to echoes of Elizabeth Bishop and William Carlos Williams. (In one poem, 'Grosse Fuge', perhaps the least successful in *Atlantis*, there are direct references to lines from Bishop and Williams.) Some of the sentiments here are too easy; in 'Description', he writes: 'I love the language/of the day's ten thousand aspects.' In 'At the Boatyard':

> What I love at the boatyard,
> at the end of Good Templar Place,
> is the scraped, accidental intensity
>
> of colour.

In 'To the Storm God': 'I love the wet ideograms/ scrawling the houseboat.' In 'Fog Argument':

> What I love
>
> is trying to see
> the furthest grassy extreme . . .

In 'Wreck': 'I love this evidence.' In 'A Letter from the Coast':

> I loved
> the flash of red excess, the cocktail dress
> and fur hat.

In some of these poems Doty is more explicit about what is happening in his life, not just in the dealing with death and wreckage, with regret ('I wish you were here') and being a lone observer, but in 'Grosse Fuge' with the arrival of a friend who is suffering from dementia. Finally, now, the word can be mentioned, the spell broken:

> *In one of these, he says, is the virus,*
> *a box of Aids. And if I open it . . .*

In the title poem he writes directly about Wally dying:

> *and I swear sometimes*
> *when I put my head to his chest*
> *I can hear the virus humming*

> *like a refrigerator.*

He writes about the dogs which he and Wally owned, and the landscape around Provincetown where they lived. The poems are competent and interesting, but the intensity and the fierce concentration are gone, and it is easy to understand why when you read *Heaven's Coast*: all the genius which Doty displays in *My Alexandria* has been transferred to this memoir, to prose rather than to the poems in *Atlantis*. *Heaven's Coast* tells the story of Doty's life with Wally and then of Wally's death: the tone is meditative, comforting, uplifting, almost religious throughout. It is hard to think of another book outside straightforward religious writing which approaches memory, death, disease, love and nature in tones of such respect and forgiveness and awe. There is something very fundamentally American about Doty: he is never prepared to give up hope that there is meaning in all of this; again and again he is prepared to ask the landscape around Provincetown to throw light on what is happening to him, to offer redemption to him and his lover. He is ready to write beautifully if he must, ready to risk everything in the distance he will push his language.

At low tide it's entirely dry, a Sahara of patterned sand and the tough green knots of sea lavender, beach grass around the edges of the beds of the tidal rivers gleaming as it bends and catches light along the straps of its leaves. As the tide mounts, twice a day, this desert disappears beneath the flood. It is a continuous apocalypse; Sahara becomes sea becomes sand again, in a theatre of furious mutability.

Some moments like this are repeated in the poems, but are almost always better in prose. One Christmas in Boston, for example, they open the window and the wind blows the tiny flakes on the Christmas tree all over the room. In the poem 'Chanteuse' this becomes:

> We were awash in
>
> a studio-sized blizzard, snow
> on your sleeves and hair, and anything
> that divided us then was bridged
>
> by the sudden graceful shock
> of being inside the warmest storm.

In *Heaven's Coast*:

We were englobed, inside the shook heart of a paperweight. Our room, which already felt outside the rush and pour of things, seemed still further set aside in space and time. In memory, that snow spins still; our laughter and our wonder in the storm's interior, lovers suddenly stunned into recognising how small what's divided and troubled them has been, how lovely their singular, flake-streaked moment is.

Although the prose book is in search of transcendence, there are also sections of plain, well-written narrative, including an account of Doty and Wally meeting and then living together in Boston, in a building which Doty revisits after Wally's death and finds almost empty ('this was a house full of gay men, in 1981, and now it's a house full of no one'), making a home together in rural Vermont against all the odds, moving to Provincetown, in love with interior decoration and planning the future. And then, in May 1989, they both took the test. Wally tested positive and began to die.

At nine o'clock on a weekday morning, late in May 1989, the public health care worker who'd come to tell us our test results blasted the world apart.

Doty writes with great subtlety and care about the process of dying, seeking to surround every possible moment with a halo.

Provincetown, 1990. The universe, God, the essence of benevolence gives us the unmatchable autumn of our lives: brilliant days brimming with warm October light that seem never to end.

Wally is slowly becoming paralysed; he does not suffer from most of the illnesses normally associated with AIDS. A few times Doty is in a rage with doctors; he writes well about the innumerable helpers who come. Always the dogs and the salt marsh and the sea offer him great comfort; but there is something intensely fragile about the solace he gets from writing itself, or from being in New England, or from reading Rilke or Cavafy or the Book of Job. There is a continuous striving in the book to keep blackness and despair at bay, and thus the reader feels their proximity. That nature is blank and offers no comfort, that the virus has no meaning beyond causing meaningless suffering, that death is a black hole, these possibilities remain all the closer to the page for not being entertained.

Heaven's Coast: A Memoir by Mark Doty, Cape

Atlantis by Mark Doty, Cape

GOODBYE TO
CATHOLIC
IRELAND

SOMETIME IN THE EARLY SIXTIES, WHEN I WAS EIGHT OR nine, the actor Micheál MacLiammóir came to Enniscorthy, a small town in the south-east of Ireland where we lived, to perform his one-man show *The Importance of Being Oscar*. My uncle, who was a staunch member of Fianna Fáil, the ruling party, and a fervent member of the ruling church – he was later decorated by the Pope – bought us all tickets, and we attended, as did many others in the town, in a family group. MacLiammóir was, we were told, a great actor, a great Gaelic speaker and a great Irishman. I remember his voice and his presence on the stage; I remember him reclining like a large sleek cat on a *chaise-longue*, world-weary and knowing and infinitely melancholy, and then standing up and looking at us all, caressing us with his narrowed eyes and speaking as though he was telling us fresh gossip, insinuations he would be asking us to keep secret at least until we had left the theatre. It was strong stuff for a small boy.

By that time, MacLiammóir had performed his one-man show all over the world, and now he was trying it out in rural Ireland. Enniscorthy was important for him: it was here in June 1927 that he met his life-long partner Hilton Edwards. They became Ireland's most famous homosexual couple. I remember, on Micheál's seventieth birthday in 1969, watching them being treated as such on Irish television. When he died in 1978, MacLiammóir's funeral was attended by the President, the Taoiseach, five government ministers and the Leader of the Opposition. He had become a national treasure.

I wondered why no one walked out of that show in Enniscorthy in the early Sixties, why it was not denounced or indeed stopped by the priests in the town. A one-man show about Oscar Wilde was surely dangerous territory in a provincial part of an over-whelmingly Catholic country. It was not as though the town was especially liberal. I remember that in these same years two men in their twenties who worked together in the same small shop in the town were also living together. I remember someone whispering to me that they were queers, and then later hearing that they had been packed off to jail again for misbehaving. Their lives were ruined. It was clear to me as I grew into my teens that being gay in this country would require care and attention.

In his essay 'Inventing Micheál MacLiammóir' in *Sex, Nation and Dissent in Irish Writing*, Éibhear Walshe makes clear that MacLiammóir and Hilton Edwards, who directed him in the show, were very careful and attentive indeed. MacLiammóir stood back from Wilde: he was the narrator of Wilde's story – he did not impersonate him, except maybe by implication. 'MacLiammóir,' Walshe writes, 'keeps all his sexual references gender-specific. In the first half of the presentation, Wilde's passion for Lillie Langtry and his love for Constance, his wife, is recounted.' And in the second half, the trial had already taken place, and thus Wilde's suffering in prison and in exile could be concentrated on – 'rendered with pathos and melodrama', as Walshe writes.

That was why it was a show for all of the family: it proceeded though winks and nods, suggestions and implications. No one knew then that MacLiammóir, who spoke Irish in the most beautiful tones, had not an Irish bone in his body. He came from England to Ireland in 1917 and he recreated himself as an actor and illustrator. He learned an Irish accent, just as many Irish people would learn English accents. In his one-man show, he proved, however, that he understood something very fundamental about the nature of discretion and indiscretion in Catholic Ireland. He had become one of us.

The best accounts of Irish Catholicism are the sociologist Micheál Mac Gréil's *Prejudice and Tolerance in Ireland* (1977) and *Prejudice in Ireland Revisited* (1996), and *The Moral Monopoly: The Catholic Church in Modern Irish Society* by Tom Inglis, published in 1987. According to Mac Gréil, more than ninety-four per cent of the population of the Republic of Ireland profess themselves to be Catholic; of these, more than eighty-one per cent attend weekly mass. More than eighty-three per cent of the population believe that religion has 'helped' them, and about the same number believe that children should be brought up in the same religion as their parents; seventy-one per cent pray once a day or more often; seventy-eight per cent agree that 'there is a God who occupies himself with every human being personally' (the same questions, when put to a Dutch sample, had forty-three per cent agreeing). Seventy-five per cent of Catholics would welcome the news that their daughter wanted to become a nun, seventy-nine per cent would welcome the news that their son wanted to become a priest.

I found Mac Gréil's first *Prejudice and Tolerance in Ireland* wonderful entertainment when I returned to live in Ireland in 1978. It was usually best after several strong drinks. (More than forty per cent of Dubliners, for example, believed at that time that skinheads should be deported.) In his second 1996 study, he shows in a survey about social distance that only 12.5 per cent of Irish people would welcome a gay person into their family, only fourteen per cent as next-door neighbours, only fifteen per cent as co-workers; fifteen per cent would, in fact, debar or deport gay people from Ireland.

Tom Inglis's book deals with the ways in which Catholicism took root in Ireland. 'It was peculiar to Ireland,' he wrote,

and it was to have a lasting effect, that the whole civilising process took place in and through the

Catholic Church. Due to the absence of a native rural bourgeoisie, the priests and later the nuns and brothers, were the most accessible and acceptable models of modern civilised behaviour.

In his chapter on 'The Irish Mother', Inglis shows how, by the middle of the nineteenth century, the mother came to represent the power of the Church in the home. Deprived of economic power, she was given immense moral authority.

The way for the mother to obtain the priest's blessing and approval was to bring up her children within the limits that he had laid down . . . In doing so she was able to call upon him as an ally in her attempts to limit what her husband and children did and said.

Almost everything that happened to me as a child was explained in Inglis's book. My mother was in charge of the nightly rosary, calling everyone in, making us kneel up, stopping my father laughing, adding prayer after prayer to the end of the five mysteries. This was her work. It seemed natural then, it was what every mother did, no father led the family rosary; they meekly took part, like the rest of us. And there was an extraordinary sense of spectacle at Sunday Mass in Pugin's cathedral, built in the town in the middle of the nineteenth century. Inglis explains that it was the place where people first learned to turn up on time, to remain silent, to have manners, to show respect. What the English learned in factories, we learned in Catholic churches. Inglis explained that Catholicism was not simply a faith which endured but a fundamental force that shaped Irish society, dominated the way we dealt with our families, the way we gathered as a group, to take just two examples.

Mary Kenny, in what she calls 'a social, personal and cultural history from the fall of Parnell to the realm of Mary Robinson', uses as her main source a devotional monthly called the *Irish Messenger of the Sacred Heart*, which had a circulation of 300,000 in 1920 and is still coming out now with a rather reduced circulation; she uses this with great skill and a certain ingenuity to show the shifts in attitude to nationalism and dogma over the past hundred years. She dismisses Tom Inglis as 'left-wing', but does not manage to disagree with his analysis in any serious way. She claims that he sees the partnership between priest and mother in Ireland as 'sinister', but this is to misrepresent the cool, detached, almost po-faced tone of his book. Her own style, on the other hand, is chatty, opinionated, personal, quirky, slightly wound-up.

Catholicism has been the central element in all the public events in the south of Ireland this century. Even though the Church opposed paramilitary activity, all of those who took part in the 1916 Rising spent their last hours in the arms of the Church. Mary Kenny has an important chapter called '1916 and the Spirit of Sacrifice'. 'It was the word-of-mouth excitement about the holiness of the 1916 rebels which seems to have meant so much to the people,' she writes. 'The men of 1916 died with fortitude and great piety . . .

The deaths of the 1916 men were told and retold as perfect Christian parables.' She quotes Conor Cruise O'Brien, who points out that the emphasis on the Catholic nature of the Rising made the partition of Ireland almost inevitable. But she is right to believe that the great turnaround in public opinion about the Rising between 1916 and 1918 had much to do with the well-publicised piety of the leaders as they faced death.

The apotheosis of holy, Catholic Ireland took place during the Eucharistic Congress in Dublin in 1932. 'A banner in a Dublin street proclaimed 23 June 1932 – the day on which the Eucharistic Congress effectively began – as "The Greatest Day in Irish History",' Kenny writes. She cites G.K. Chesterton, who met a woman on a Dublin tram during the Congress. 'Well, if it rains now,' she said, 'He'll have brought it on Himself.' Chesterton saw a banner hanging between two tenement houses: 'God Bless Christ the King,' it said.

From then on an authoritarian Church and a fragile, insecure State combined to produce a sort of dark ages. It was as though Ireland north and south vied with each other over who could produce the most sectarian state. Censorship, mass emigration, economic stagnation. For several chapters this book deals not with the Church but with the State, because the Church was the State. It has always been clear that neutrality in the war made Ireland insular, self-obsessed and uneasy with itself. Kenny is correct when she writes that 'neutrality in the Second World War was widely, indeed overwhelmingly, supported by the people of Eire, as Catholic Ireland was called before it became a Republic in 1949.' She goes on:

> In the end, the political rigidity of this time was greatly to Ireland's disadvantage. For the wartime censorship deprived people of information about the moral aspect of a conflict which has, perhaps, marked our century more than any other event. To this day, I think, many Irish people are not really aware of how strongly it has formed neighbouring European nations.

The impulse towards neutrality had much in common with the Church's view of its own authority. Everything must be controlled and held; joining Britain in the fight against Hitler would have been to admit that Britain could possibly have right on its side, could be, under certain circumstances, a moral arbiter. This would have been simply impossible in Ireland in 1939: it would have been to admit that taking up arms in Ireland between 1916 and 1922 was perhaps a mistake, or something that should now be forgotten. Similarly, for the Church to loosen its hold on its flock would, the Church believed, have led to people abandoning the Church, turning away from religion.

One version of the history of Irish Catholicism after the foundation of the state is not a history of prayer and devotion, of mass-going and vocations: it is a history of coercion and control. The figure who emerges from it most strongly is John Charles McQuaid, the

Archbishop of Dublin between 1940 and 1972, who stopped Noel Browne, the Minister for Health in 1951, from introducing a health scheme for mothers, thereby bringing down the Government, and who insisted that John McGahern be fired from his job as a teacher in 1965 when his novel *The Dark* had been banned. (*The Dark* mentioned masturbation, at that time, and perhaps even still, the national pastime, and used the word 'fuck' on the first page.)

Mary Kenny devotes chapters to the relationship between the Church and the rise of feminism, the violence in the North and the referenda on moral issues in the Republic. She makes sweeping statements, she quotes from books, she makes reference to the period at the end of the Sixties when she was women's editor of the *Irish Press* and, it is said, the wildest girl in Dublin. Sometimes, she quotes interesting statistics. In 1970 there were fewer than two thousand deserted wives in the Republic: by 1994 there were almost sixteen thousand. In 1970 there were seven marriages per 1000 people: in 1994 this had fallen to 4.4. In 1970 there were twenty-one births per thousand people; by 1993, it had gone down to 13.9.

In 1970 Mary Kenny was living in Ireland: by 1994 she had been in London for more than twenty years. It is notoriously difficult to follow what is going on in Ireland from outside. Her account of the last twenty years lack subtlety and detail. While, for example, the Church has become more easy-going in public, it has become stricter in private on certain issues. Teachers of Christian doctrine are monitored much more closely now in Catholic schools. Parents of children who are making First Communion and Confirmation are forced to become involved. If you want to get married in a Catholic church, you have to attend a Catholic marriage guidance course, and these, I am told, are excruciating. There were for many years two children's hospitals in Dublin, one Catholic, one Protestant; several attempts to merge them failed because the Catholic Church would not cede any rights to what they call 'another ethos'. When I asked a senior doctor on the Catholic side why the Church cared so much about this, he explained that it had to do with counselling: in the Catholic hospital parents who wanted to know whether they were likely to have a handicapped child would have to be told that abortion was not an option. But it was, he said, essentially about control. In another hospital in Dublin controlled by nuns, promotion was refused to doctors, including doctors at the top of their profession, who supported the free availability of contraceptives.

The Church has lost the war against contraception and divorce, and won the battle, at least for the moment, on abortion. But it still works its authority when it can. It won the right to have certain people – teachers and nurses mainly – excluded from recent anti-discrimination legislation, on the basis that the Church as an employer has a right to discriminate against those who do not support its ethos.

In the end, the explosion in the Irish Church came from within. When the news broke that the Bishop of Galway had fathered a son and, in Kenny's words,

'deserted and denied mother and child', Mary Kenny
felt that she at first took the matter too lightly.
'Think of the Borgia Popes,' she said jokingly to an
editor in Dublin. 'During these events,' she writes
here,

> I used to hear people in Ireland say: 'It can't get
> worse.' And each time it did. On one Monday in
> November 1994, the three leading stories on RTE
> television were the political repercussions following
> the Brendan Smyth [the priest who had abused a
> large number of young people] case, the collapse and
> death of the Dublin priest in a homosexual sauna
> club [as chance would have it, there were two other
> priests on the premises to give him the last rites] and
> the conviction of the Galway priest for a sexual
> assault on a young man. In one news bulletin. I made
> no more jokes about Renaissance Popes or the
> Church being for sinners. The wave upon wave of
> charges and convictions were relentless, squalid and
> depressing.

As these cases broke in Ireland, I watched them
carefully, and I wished that I could draw a conclusion, but I could not. It would be easy to say that
these men had grown up in a time when the Church
could do exactly what it wanted – stop legislation,
bring down governments, fire novelists from their
jobs – and it was therefore easy for them to think that
they could do what they wanted. But it wasn't like
that. Between the ages of fifteen and seventeen, I went

to a diocesan school run by priests, which had a seminary attached. From that time I know five priests who have been – what can I call it? – in the news. One is in jail in the North; one received a suspended sentence, one fled to another jurisdiction; two are facing serious charges.

If you had shone a light on each face around the church – there were more than three hundred of us – during evening Benediction in that school and seminary, there would be no reason why you would fix on these five people. What each one did was different, was done over a different period of time; but all of them, as far as I am aware, were interested in teenage boys. In the case of four of them, it never occurred to me when I first knew them that they were gay. Even with the fifth, it seemed an impossible idea. I believe that they joined the Church sincerely; perhaps the idea that they had no sexual interest in women made them feel they had a vocation – there was no one to tell them otherwise, these things were not discussed. Two of them had been priests for a long time when they made headlines; the other three were just starting their careers. They destroyed people's lives; they abused their responsibility.

It is probable that had they not been gay they would not have joined the seminary. When they joined the seminary no one talked about homosexuality, it was not allowed for as a possibility. No one gave these men any guidance about their sexuality; in the society around them it was a great taboo, and still is, as Mac Gréil's survey makes clear. I know how long the evenings must have been for them. I know how long they must have denied it, and, when they gave into it, how afraid they must have been. I know how much damage they caused. I imagine it was a lonely old business being gay in that seminary and perhaps worse afterwards in the outside world. Recently, I met someone whose brother had been propositioned by one of these priests. 'He deserves to be in jail just for that,' the man said to me.

In the scale of social distance in the Republic of Ireland, only five groups came below gay people: they are members of Sinn Fein, followers of Hare Krishna, people with AIDS (whom 22.5 per cent of those surveyed would debar or deport from Ireland), drug addicts and members of the Provisional IRA (whom 43.1 per cent would deport or debar). It is likely that priests 'in the news' would now be lower on the scale.

In contrast, the writers who figure in Éibhear Walshe's *Sex, Nation and Dissent in Irish Writing* seem oddly heroic as they grappled, and still grapple, in public with the topic which was, and is, more dangerous in Ireland than any other: sexual difference, sexual ambiguity. Since very little explicitly lesbian writing exists, it is necessary here to look at the work of certain women writers – Eva Gore Booth, Edith Somerville and Violet Martin, Elizabeth Bowen, Molly Keane, each of whom has her own chapter – and how they dealt with same-sex love. Some of these women were, as far as we know, gay; others were not. The issues are clearer in other essays – in Éibhear Walshe's piece on Mac Liammóir, for example, or Lillis Ó

Laoire's on the poetry of Cathel Ó Searchaigh, some of which is explicitly gay, or Anne Fogarty's on two works of fiction which have lesbian characters, Kate O'Brien's *As Music and Splendour* and Mary Dorcey's *A Noise from the Woodshed*.

It is possible that Cathal Ó Searchaigh is not the first gay poet in the Irish language; Gaelic poems in the eighteenth and nineteenth centuries are full of unrequited and impossible love, and it is certainly possible that some of them were written by a man about a man. But Ó Searchaigh is the first poet in a long tradition to be explicit about his sexuality. One of his poems has been on the school curriculum, and many teachers believed that it was a man's love poem to a woman, rather than to a man, but in the last few years especially Ó Searchaigh has made his position very clear – 'we were too poor to have closets' was his line – as does the Introduction to the 1993 bilingual version of his selected poems.

It is unlikely that any of the subjects in Éibhear Walshe's book paid much attention to the *Irish Messenger of the Sacred Heart* or in 1932 were overjoyed at the prospect of the Eucharistic Congress. On the other hand, Mary Kenny and her cast of Catholics would probably not be much concerned about finding a lesbian tradition, so that students and readers could know that within the monolith, or not far away from it, there were individuals who had other things on their minds. On the evidence which Micheál Mac Gréil presents us, it is clear that the Catholic Church will not go away; the vast majority of citizens of the

Republic are likely to remain Catholic. It is useful to remind them now and then of the people they have for so long sought to exclude and marginalise.

Sex, Nation and Dissent in Irish Writing edited by Éibhear Walshe, Cork

Goodbye to Catholic Ireland by Mary Kenny, Sinclair-Stevenson

ACKNOWLEDGEMENTS

I am grateful to the *London Review of Books* for persisting with me, to Mary Kay Wilmers and Andrew O'Hagan, John Lanchester, Jean McNicol, Jeremy Harding and Daniel Soar, and also to Brendan Barrington at the *Dublin Review*, where the chapter on Francis Bacon first appeared, and to Graydon Carter, Wayne Lawson and Beatrice Monti at *Vanity Fair* who commissioned the chapter on Pedro Almodóvar. The chapters on Oscar Wilde and James Baldwin were written while I was a Fellow at the Center for Scholars and Writers at the New York Public Library. I am grateful to my colleagues there for, among other things, much stimulating discussion; and to Peter Gay, the Director of the Center, and Pamela Leo and Rachael Kafrissen for all their kindness. Also thanks to Catriona Crowe, Eileen Ahearn, Aidan Dunne and George O'Brien for advice and support. And to Nikki Christer and Christine Mattey at Picador in Sydney, Peter Straus at Picador in London and Caradoc King at A. P. Watt in London for their kindness and encouragement.